Pattern Block Book

Table of Contents

Introduction

Background

Pattern blocks are one of the most familiar and available hands-on materials in the elementary school classroom today. It is widely accepted by most educators that learning mathematical concepts through exploration with manipulatives should be an integral piece of any instructional program for children.

In the past twenty years, both state and national standards have emerged for the teaching of elementary mathematics. The standards are generally intended to help children develop a strong conceptual framework while encouraging and developing skills and the natural inclination to solve problems. These standards outline specific areas of instruction that are much the same from state-to-state and often form the basis of formal assessment programs. This book is designed to provide teachers with effective ways to use pattern blocks to address the major topics of the math standards. Thus, it is organized into exactly the same strands:

- Number and Operations
- Measurement
- Geometry
- Algebra
- Statistics and Probability

Suggestions for the Classroom

Before plunging into the activities, allow ample time for children to explore with the pattern blocks. In addition to satisfying their natural curiosity, this will build confidence and familiarity that will smooth the way for new terms, ideas and challenges. In that all children absorb and learn differently, this is a good time to observe and consider the ways that each child uses the pattern blocks.

If possible, have a set of overhead pattern blocks (and projector) on hand to model the activities when appropriate. Invite students to show their work on the overhead and lead discussions about outcomes. For a whole class, about 4 complete sets of 250 pattern blocks will be needed. To make them easier to handle, each set can be broken into 4 subsets and put into resealable bags.

As with any manipulative, it is important for the teacher to act as a guide. At first, refer to the pattern blocks by color. As children become familiar with the shapes, use the names in combination with the color if necessary. Many activities may generate a range of correct answers; students should be encouraged to predict outcomes and discuss their reasoning. It is helpful to ask questions when children get stuck enabling them to learn how to problem solve.

Assessment and Instruction

To ensure that progress is being made in meeting the standards covered in this book, use the Focal Point Progress sheet to record observations about student performance. It is useful to note the date reviewed and the level of proficiency for each item. Of course, for Kindergarten students you will not have the same expectation of performance against each focal point as for upper grades. This is meant to provide a road-map for instruction. The focal point is clearly described at the start of each lesson.

Example

	Needs Instruction	Working at Level
	10/15	3/12

In this example, the student needed instruction on October 15 and became proficient with the focal point on March 12.

PATTERN BLOCK
BOOK

Sandra Pryor Clarkson and Vincent J. Altamuro

www.didax.com

Layout and Illustration: Christopher Michon
Project Advisor: Maggie Holler

Printed in the United States of America.

This book is printed on recycled paper.

Order Number 2-5294
ISBN 978-1-58324-276-6

B C D E F 12 11 10 09 08

395 Main Street
Rowley, MA 01969
www.didax.com

Focal Point Progress Sheet

Name: _____

Use the right-hand column to mark the date reviewed and level of proficiency.

Focal Point Outcome	Needs Instruction	Working at Level
Identifies constant properties like color, shape and size		
Identifies variable properties like orientation, ordination and juxtaposition		
Matches shapes with different sizes and the same orientation		
Recognizes and names shapes		
Understands concept of equivalency in shapes		
Counts a set of objects greater than one and less than 10		
Recognizes and names sets		
Groups in ones and tens		
Uses a table to describe patterns		
Uses informal counting strategies		
Identifies angles as corners of a polygon; identifies sides of a polygon; sorts shapes according to the number of angles and sides		
Distinguishes between points on the inside and outside of a geometric shape		
Understands concept of symmetry		
Understands concept of perimeter		
Identifies right angles		
Identifies, duplicates and extends patterns		
Uses patterns to solve simple equations		
Represents measurements and discrete data in picture and bar graphs		
Uses attributes of color, shape or number to determine membership in a set		

Pattern Block Book

Explore & Discover

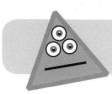

Explore & Discover: **Turn About**

Materials

- One block of each color

Instructions

Ask the students to place the pattern blocks in the outlines in the column on the left. Then have them move the blocks one at a time from the left column to the appropriate outlines in the right column.

Guided Learning

1. Name each piece by color and shape.

    Yellow hexagon, red trapezoid, blue rhombus, green triangle, orange square, tan rhombus

2. How is each pattern block the same before and after moving it?

    Color and shape stay the same

3. How is each pattern block different before and after moving it?

    Different orientation made by turning block; different ordinal position—first on left, 6th on right side, etc.; different neighbors

Explore More with PB!

Ask the students to use the pattern blocks to make an original design. Have them name the blocks used and describe their placement.

Turn About

PLACE   **MOVE**

Explore & Discover: **Slip and Slide**

Focal Point

Geometry – Describing shapes and space.

Identify constant properties like color, shape and size. Identify variable properties like orientation, ordination and juxtaposition. Identify transformations like turn, slide and flip; match shapes with same sizes and different orientation.

Materials

- One block of each color

Instructions

Place the pattern blocks in the outlined spaces in the rooster on the left. Move the blocks one at a time onto the spaces in the chick at the right of the page.

Guided Learning

1. Name each piece by color and shape.

   Yellow hexagon, red trapezoid, blue rhombus, green triangle, orange square, tan rhombus

2. How is each pattern block the same before and after moving it?

   Color and shape stay the same

3. How did you have to change each block to move it from the rooster to the chick?

   Turn, slide, flip

Explore More with PB!

Ask the students to make a new original design in the picture frame. Record the new design by using a pattern block template or by tracing around the blocks. Have the students explain their designs.

Slip and Slide

Name: _____

PLACE   **MOVE**

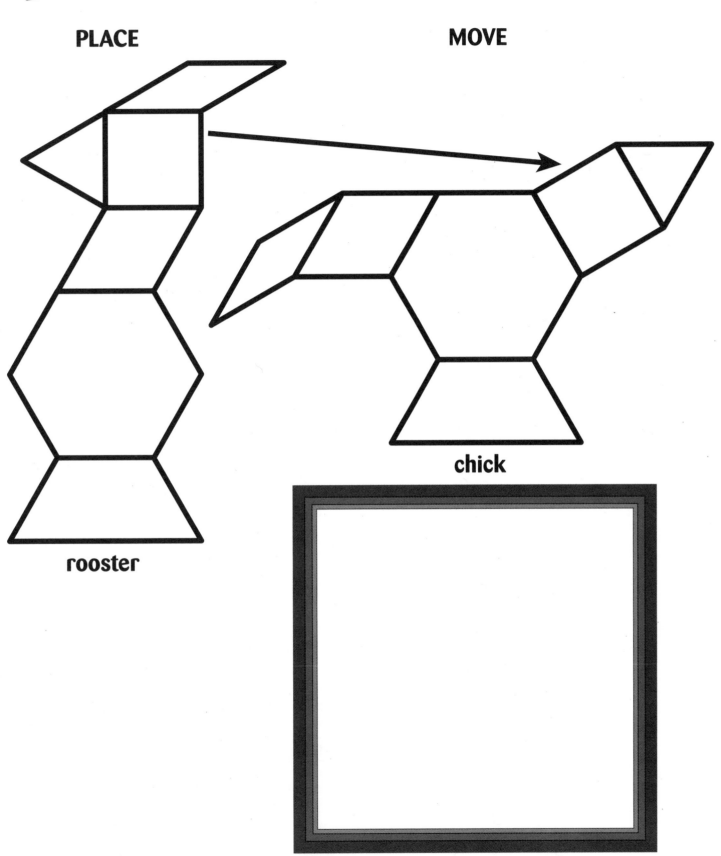

rooster

chick

Explore & Discover: **Take One**

Focal Point

Geometry – Identifying shapes and describing spatial relationships.

Identify constant properties like color, shape and size. Identify variable properties like orientation, ordination and juxtaposition. Explain to others how the problem is solved, sharing strategies.

Materials

• One block of each color

Instructions

Ask the students to use the pattern blocks to make the lion. Then have them fill in each of the other figures with pattern blocks.

Guided Learning

1. Name each piece by color and shape.

   Yellow hexagon, red trapezoid, blue rhombus, green triangle, orange square, tan rhombus

2. Explain how you knew how to place the shapes.

3. Which shapes did you place first? Why?

Explore More with PB!

Have the students use the same six blocks and make their own designs. They can then outline the design and ask a classmate to fill it in with blocks.

Name: _____

TAKE

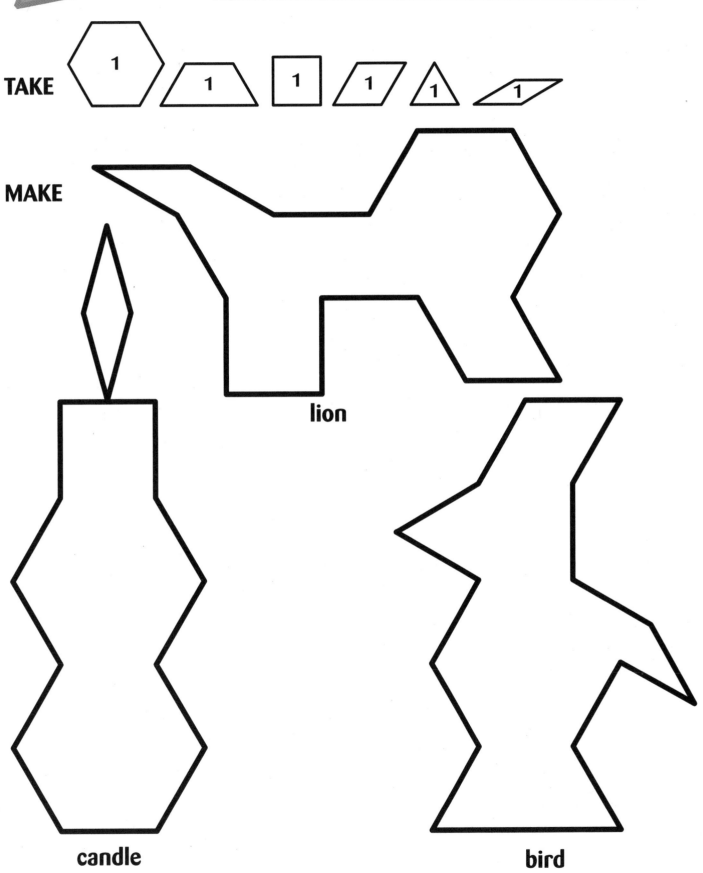

MAKE

lion

candle

bird

Explore & Discover: **Copy Cats**

Focal Point

Geometry – Composing and decomposing geometric shapes.

Identify constant properties like color, shape and size. Identify variable properties like orientation, ordination and juxtaposition. Complete the puzzle using spatial-visual ideas by composing two dimensional shapes. Match shapes with same sizes and orientation.

Materials

- One block of each color
- One additional triangle

Instructions

Have students choose the pattern blocks needed to cover the shape on the left. Then ask them to cover the shape on the right with the same pattern blocks. They should repeat for each shape. The last shape will be constructed without using an outline.

If students have trouble, provide the following hints:

1. Place the pattern blocks in the appropriate spaces in the shape on the left.
2. Move blocks one at a time from the shape on the left to the shape on the right.
3. Trace around the blocks.

Guided Learning

1. Name each piece by color and shape.

   Yellow hexagon, red trapezoid, blue rhombus, green triangle, orange square, tan rhombus

2. How is each pattern block the same before and after moving it?

   Color, shape and position stay the same

3. How is each pattern block different after moving it?

   There is no difference, the shapes are in the same position on the right as they were on the left

Explore More with PB!

Allow students to use additional pattern blocks as needed to fill in the figures on the right in a different way. Students may work in pairs. One student builds a design with 4 or 5 blocks and then the partner copies it. Use overhead pattern blocks to create designs that students may copy at their desks.

Name: _____

LOOK   **COPY**

Explore & Discover: **From Little to Big**

Focal Point

Geometry – Describing and analyzing properties of two-dimensional shapes.

Reproduce a figure from a reduced size pattern or template. Match shapes with different sizes and the same orientation.

Materials

- Pattern blocks

Instructions

Tell the students to look carefully at the first design on the left and to take the pattern blocks needed. Then they are to copy the design, making a similar design on the right in the outline provided, repeating for each design.

Guided Learning

1. What method did you use to fill in the large outlines?

Explore More with PB!

On the board or on an overhead projector, present additional designs, drawing or using overhead pattern blocks. Ask the student to copy the design on a blank page. Students may create their own designs on the overhead projector for classmates to copy at their desks.

Name: _____

LOOK

COPY

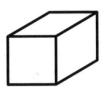

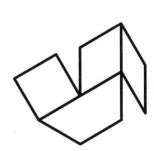

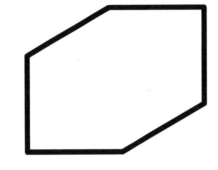

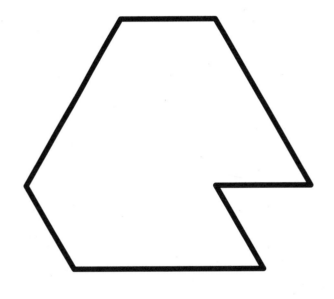

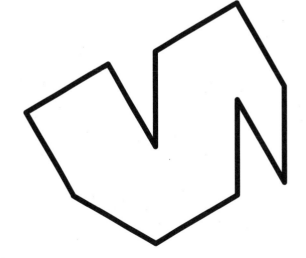

Explore & Discover: **Kites**

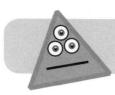

Focal Point

Geometry – Describing and analyzing properties of two-dimensional shapes.

Investigate two dimensional shapes by covering the shapes with various combinations of pattern block pieces.

Materials

- Pattern blocks

Instructions

Ask the student to place the blocks on the kites, one at a time, in order (Kite A, B and then C). They can cover Kite D in any manner they choose. Have them record the number of each kind of block used for Kite D.

Guided Learning

1. Which kite needed the fewest blocks? The most?
2. Why do the number of triangles vary?
3. Can you make a kite with no triangles?
4. Can you make a kite with only red blocks?

Explore More with PB!

Students may use overhead pattern blocks to show their kites. Discuss the different arrangements of the blocks. Discuss the different ways students covered Kite D.

Name: _____

COVER WITH:

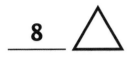

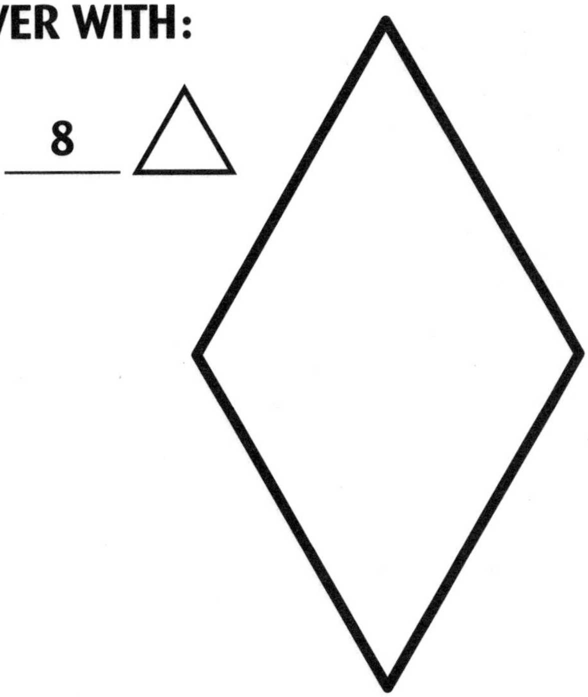

___8___

Kite A

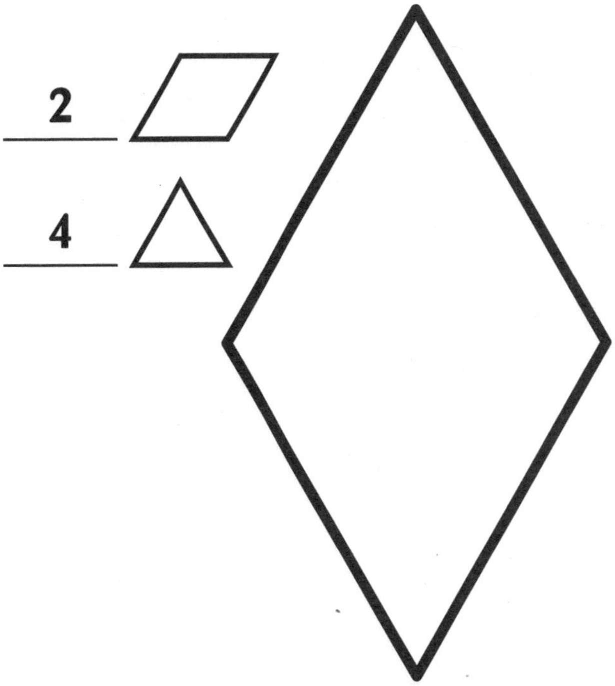

___2___ ▱

___4___ △

Kite B

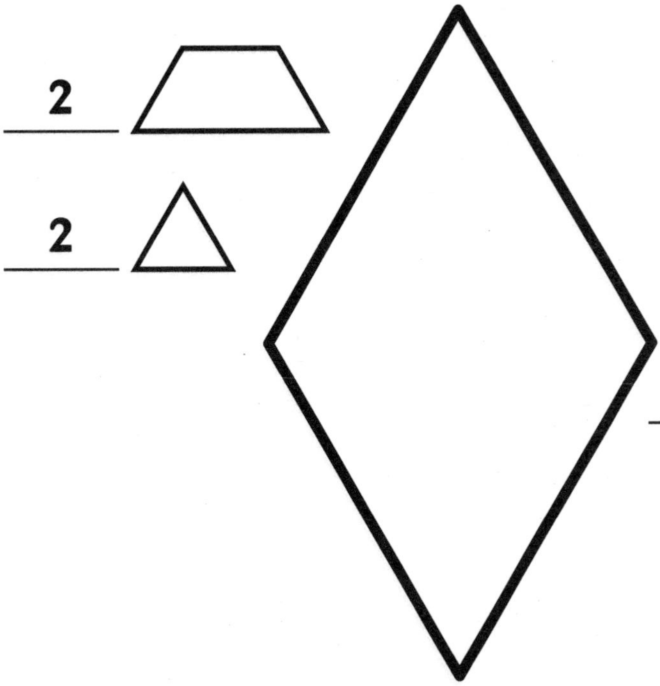

___2___ ▱ (trapezoid)

___2___ △

Kite C

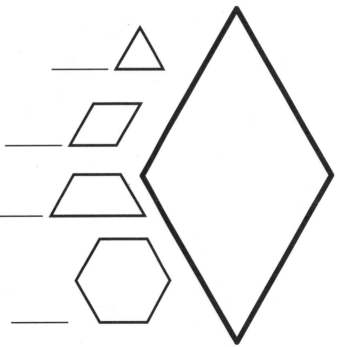

Kite D

Focal Point

Geometry – Describing and analyzing properties of two-dimensional shapes.

Predict what is needed and verify the prediction, recognizing that mathematical ideas need to be supported by evidence.

Materials

- Pattern blocks

Instructions

Students may work individually or in pairs. Ask them to cover the dinosaur with any combination of pattern blocks. Then have them remove the pieces and try to make a dinosaur using only one color. If they can fill in the dinosaur ask them to indicate "Yes" on the line; if not they will fill in the "No" blank. On the grid below, ask students to make their own dinosaur using only red trapezoids and then outline the figure.

Guided Learning

1. Do you think that the dinosaur can be made with just one color of block?

2. Which color blocks worked? Why do you think one color will work and another won't?

3. How does the dinosaur you made below differ from the one above?

Explore More with PB!

Ask students to make 2-color dinosaurs using the same number of each color block.

Name: _____

COVER THE DINOSAUR WITH PATTERN BLOCKS.

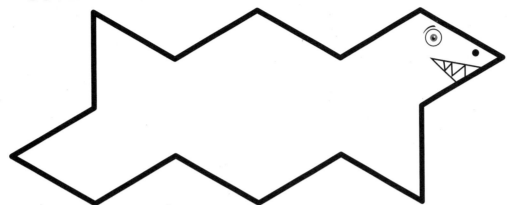

REMOVE THE PATTERN BLOCKS. NOW COVER ONLY WITH:

A. ⬡ (hexagons)   yes _____   no _____

B. ▱ (blue rhombuses)   yes _____   no _____

C. △ (triangles)   yes _____   no _____

D. ▱ (trapezoids)   yes _____   no _____

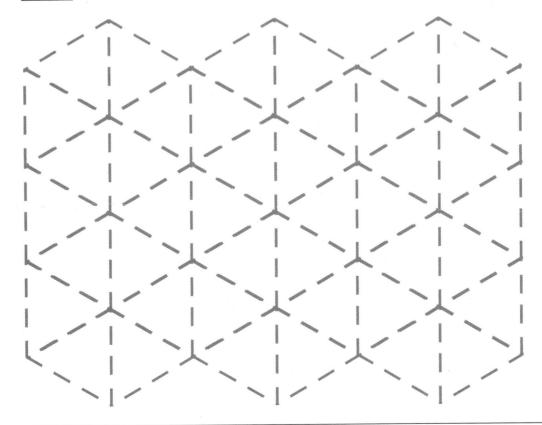

Focal Point

Geometry – Composing and decomposing geometric shapes.

Predict what is needed and verify the prediction, recognizing that mathematical ideas need to be supported by evidence. Explore guesses using manipulative materials.

Materials

- Pattern blocks

Instructions

Ask students to take the number of blocks shown. Ask them to guess which piece is missing before placing the blocks on the picture. Then they may cover the design and find the missing piece.

Guided Learning

1. Which piece is missing?
2. How do you know?
3. Was your prediction correct?

Explore More with PB!

Ask a student to show an outline of a figure she has designed to a partner and list the blocks she used minus one. The partner then guesses the missing piece before placing the blocks in the new outline.

Name: _____

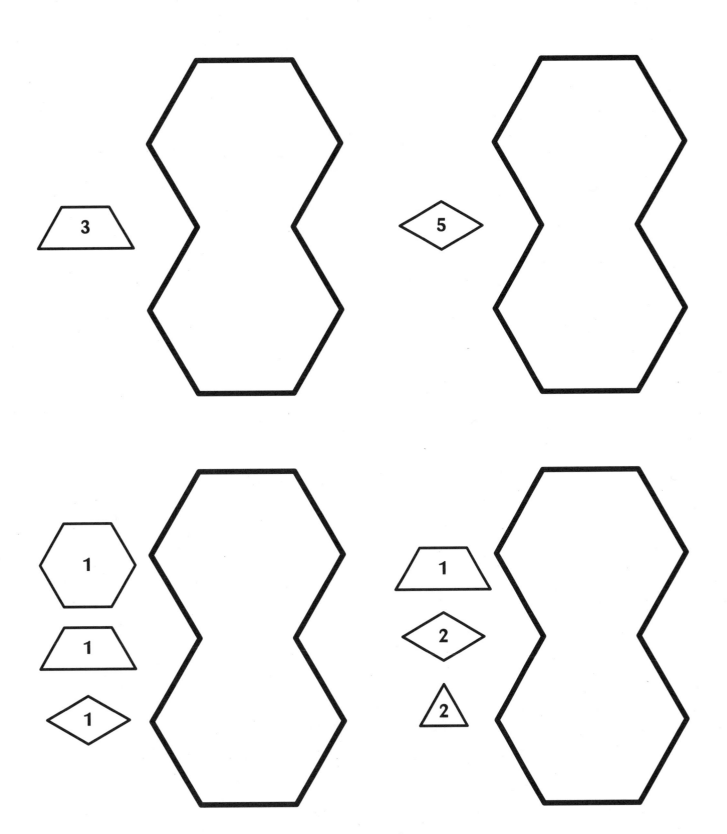

Focal Point

Geometry: Describing and analyzing properties of two-dimensional shapes.

Reproduce a picture from memory using pattern blocks. Describe the figure using appropriate mathematical language.

Materials

- Pattern blocks

Instructions

Working in pairs, ask one student to take the blocks shown. The second student studies the picture without touching the blocks. The first student counts slowly from 1 to 10; at "10" he turns the page over and gives the blocks to the second student who uses the blocks to copy the picture from memory. Then have the students swap places to complete all three figures at least once each.

Guided Learning

1. Which figures were easiest to remember?
2. In each case, which part of the design did you make first? Why?

Explore More with PB!

Have a student make an original design and slowly describe the design to a partner. The partner then tries to recreate the design. At each step, the designer should tell the partner whether the recreated design is right or wrong.

Name: _____

TAKE 3 BLOCKS

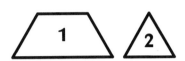

TAKE 3 BLOCKS

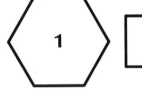 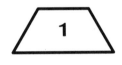

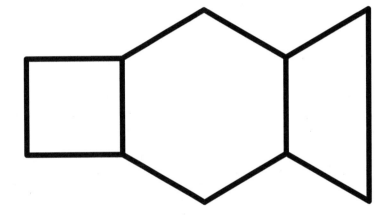

TAKE 4 BLOCKS

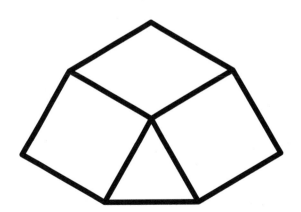

Focal Point

Geometry – Composing and decomposing geometric shapes.

Recognize and reinforce the names of geometric shapes, introducing the concept of equivalency.

Materials

- Hexagonal game boards
- A cube with red, blue and green dots on opposite sides
- Three blue pattern blocks
- Two red pattern blocks
- Six green pattern blocks

Reproduce and cut the hexagonal game boards before starting.

Instructions

Students work in pairs.

The players cover their game board hexagons using the correct color of pattern blocks. Player 1 tosses the cube and then removes one block, if possible, of the color shown on the cube face. Player 2 now tosses the cube and removes one block from his game board, if possible. Play continues to alternate as above. The first player to "unwrap" all three hexagons completely on his game board is the winner.

Guided Learning

1. What happens if you allow trading?

For example, if a player tosses the cube and the green face is shown, but the player has no green triangles to remove, he can trade one of the blue rhombuses he has for 2 green triangles. Then he will be able to remove one green triangle.

Explore More with PB!

Have the students play the game again, this time with an additional cube with the numbers 1, 2 and 3 on opposite sides. Each player removes the color and number of pieces indicated by the cube. Take turns with one roll per turn.

Unwrapping Packages

Name: _____

PLAYER 1   **blue**   **red**   **green**

PLAYER 2   **blue**   **red**   **green**

PLAYER 1   **blue**   **red**   **green**

PLAYER 2   **blue**   **red**   **green**

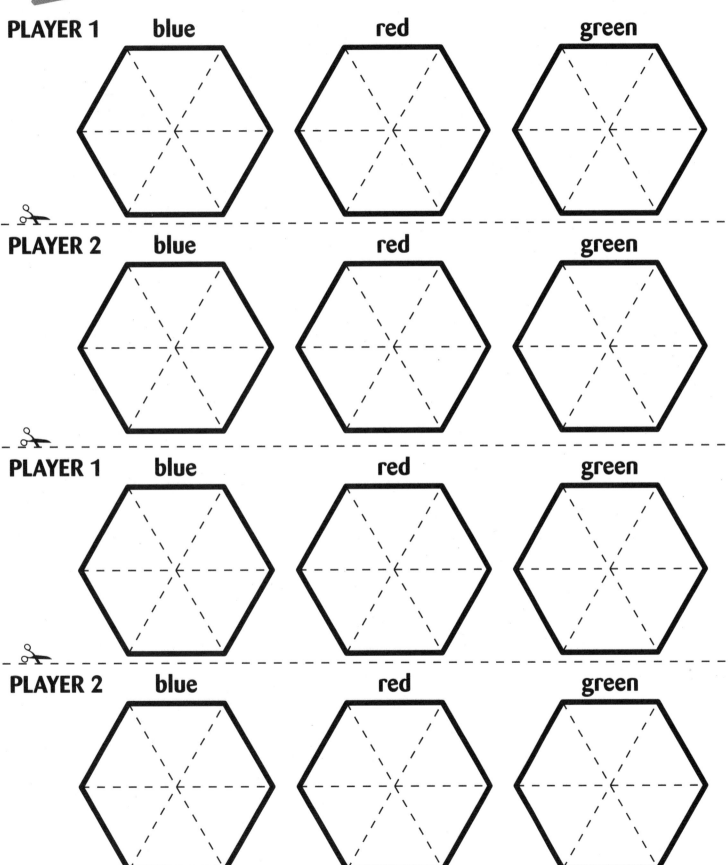

Pattern Block Book

Number & Operations

Focal Point

Number and Operations – Representing, comparing and ordering whole numbers and joining and separating sets.

Count a set of objects greater than one and less than 10 and know that the last counting word indicates how many items are in the set.

Materials

- Pattern blocks

Instructions

Ask the students to cover the design. Once they have done this, have them remove the blocks by color and shape one at a time and count the number of each block. Then they will record the number of each block in the given space.

Guided Learning

1. Name each piece by color and shape.

   Yellow hexagon, red trapezoid, blue rhombus, green triangle, orange square, tan rhombus

Explore More with PB!

Ask students to cover the picture with different blocks and repeat the activity. Which blocks did they use more of than before? Which blocks did they use fewer of than before?

Name: _____

HOW MANY?

A. ⬡ ___ ⬠ ___ ▱ ___ △ ___ ☐ ___ ◇ ___

B. ⬡ ___ ⬠ ___ ▱ ___ △ ___ ☐ ___ ◇ ___

Focal Point

Number and Operations – Representing, comparing and ordering whole numbers and joining and separating sets.

Decompose shapes, recognizing parts of a whole (breaking one shape into two parts). Investigate mathematical conjectures; explore guesses, using manipulative materials. Reinforce counting sets of objects.

Materials

• Pattern blocks

Instructions

Have students cover each design with exactly 2 pattern blocks.

Guided Learning

1. Which blocks did you use?

    Students should be able to describe pieces as well as give the color and name.

Explore More with PB!

Have the students try to cover the designs with two other blocks. Which designs can be covered in more than one way? Which designs can be covered using exactly 2 pattern blocks if the blocks are different? Which designs can be covered using exactly 2 pattern blocks if the blocks are the same?

From 1 Make 2

Name: _____

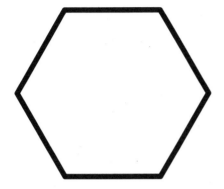

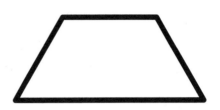

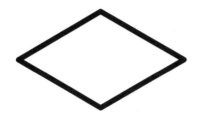

Focal Point

Number and Operations – Representing, comparing and ordering whole numbers and joining and separating sets.

Decompose shapes, recognizing parts of a whole (breaking one shape into three parts). Investigate mathematical conjectures; explore guesses, using manipulative materials. Reinforce counting sets of objects.

Materials

- Pattern blocks

Instructions

Tell the students to cover each design with exactly 3 pattern blocks.

Guided Learning

1. Name each piece by color and shape.

   Yellow hexagon, red trapezoid, blue rhombus, green triangle, orange square, tan rhombus. Students should develop mathematical language to describe the pattern blocks.

Explore More with PB!

Ask the student to try to cover the designs with 3 other blocks. Which designs can be covered in more than one way? Which designs can be covered using exactly 3 pattern blocks if the blocks are different? Which designs can be covered using the same or different blocks? Which designs can be covered with more than 3 blocks?

Name: _____

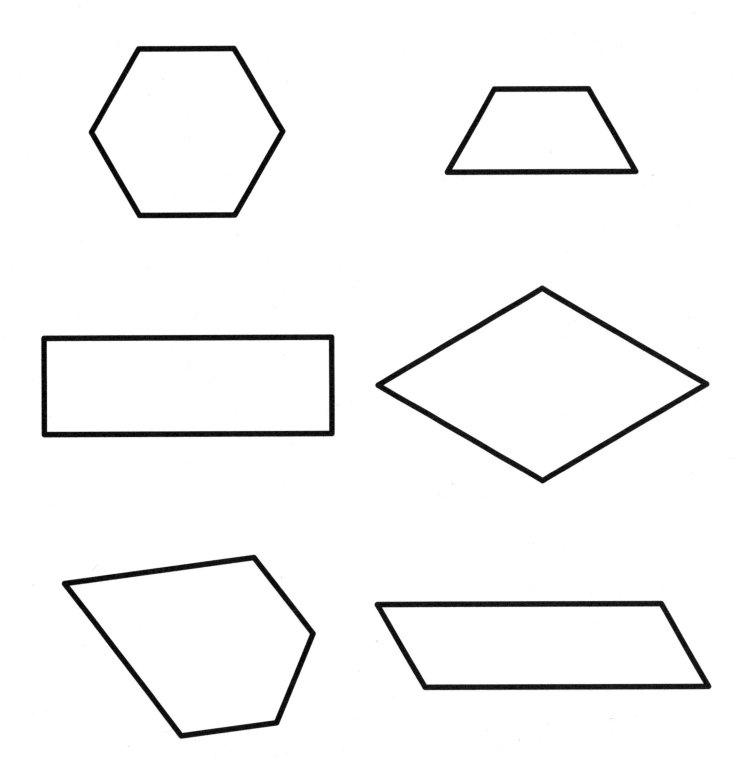

Number & Operations: **Take Four**

Focal Point

Number and Operations – Representing, comparing and ordering whole numbers and joining and separating sets.

Decompose shapes, recognizing parts of a whole (breaking one shape into four parts). Investigate mathematical conjectures; explore guesses, using manipulative materials. Reinforce counting sets of objects.

Materials

- Pattern blocks
- Crayons or colored pencils

Instructions

Ask the students to try to cover each design with exactly 4 blocks. Then have them show how they did this by drawing in figure A to show the blocks used. You may need to demonstrate. Then they should try to find another way to cover the design and illustrate this in figure B.

Guided Learning

1. How many different ways can the class cover each design?

   Allow students to share their results

Explore More with PB!
Students should attempt to cover designs with fewer than 4 blocks. Which designs will allow this?

Take Four

Name: _____

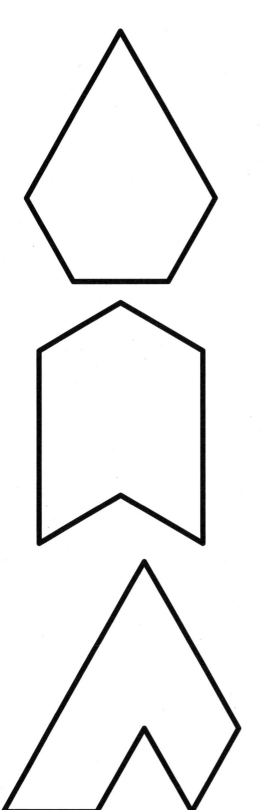

A.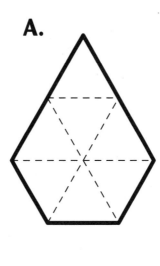

B.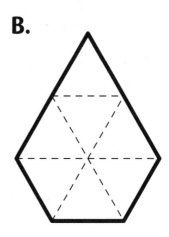

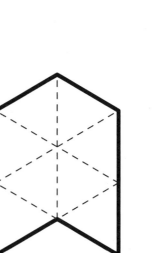

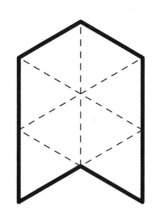

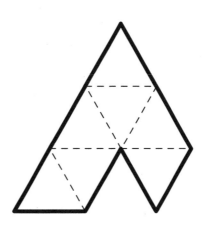

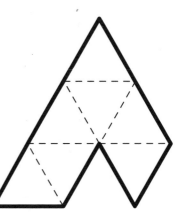

Focal Point

Number and Operations – Representing, comparing and ordering whole numbers and joining and separating sets.

Geometry – Composing and decomposing geometric shapes.

Children compose and decompose plane and solid figures (e.g., by putting two congruent isosceles triangles together to make a rhombus), thus building an understanding of part-whole relationships as well as the properties of the original and composite shapes.

Materials

- Pattern blocks
- Crayons or colored pencils

Instructions

Ask the students to try to cover each design with exactly 5 blocks. Then have them show how they did this by drawing in figure A to show the blocks used. You may need to demonstrate. Then they should try to find another way to cover the design and illustrate this in figure B.

Guided Learning

1. Discuss your strategies for filling in the designs.
2. How are solutions A and B different?
3. How many triangles cover each shape?

Explore More with PB!

Working in pairs, have partner see how many different ways can they can cover each design. For each design, can they use more than 5 blocks? What is the greatest number of blocks they need to cover each design? The fewest?

High Five

Name: _____

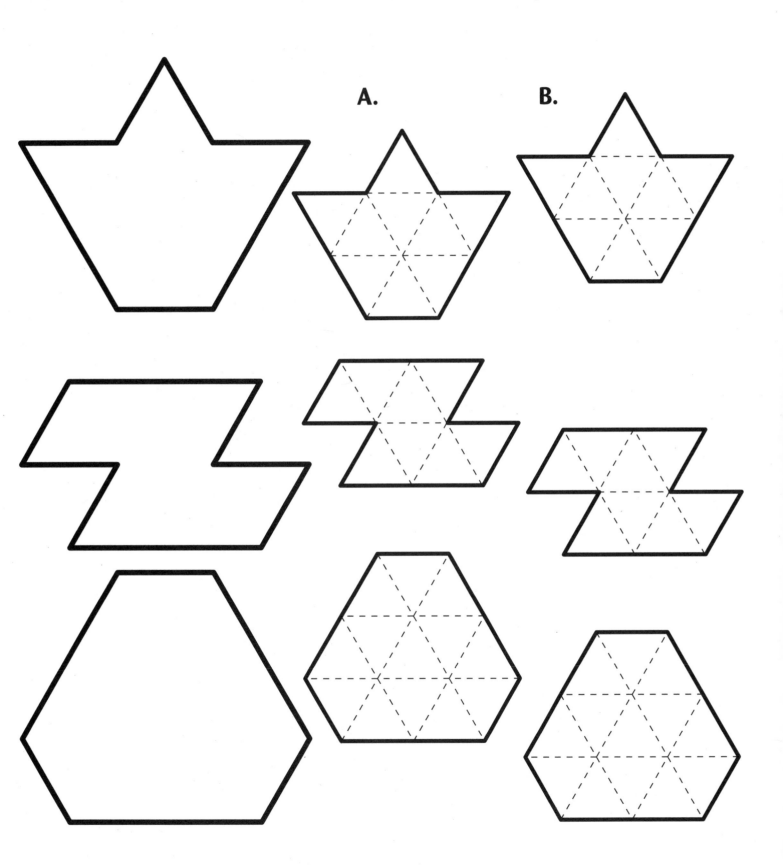

Number & Operations: **Trading Triangles**

Focal Point

Number and Operations – Developing an understanding of whole number relationships, including grouping in tens and ones.

Geometry – Composing and decomposing geometric shapes.

Materials

- Pattern blocks
- Colored pencils or crayons

Instructions/Guided Learning

Ask the students to cover design A exactly with the pattern blocks shown by the solid lines and to cover design B with triangles only.

1. How many triangles did you use altogether?

Now have students remove a rhombus from design A and remove the triangles from B that were in the place of the rhombus.

2. How many triangles replaced the rhombus?

Next, have them remove a trapezoid from design A and remove the triangles from design B that were in the place of the trapezoid.

3. How many triangles replaced the trapezoid?

4. How many triangles do you need to cover the entire design?

5. How many triangles would replace a hexagon?

Tell the students to use 10 triangles and make an original design in space C and outline it. Then have them make the same design in space D, but with fewer pattern blocks of any shape.

Explore More with PB!

Ask students to try to make a design using the fewest possible pieces (without using triangles) that can be covered exactly with 10 triangles. Have them verify their design by covering it with 10 triangles.

Trading Triangles

Name: _____

cover with △

A.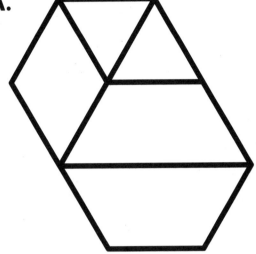

B.

▱ = _____ △   ⬠ = _____ △   ⬡ = _____ △

C.	**D.**
your own design	**your own design**

Focal Point

Number and Operations – Developing an understanding of whole number relationships, including grouping in tens and ones.

Geometry – Composing and decomposing geometric shapes.

Materials

- Pattern blocks

Instructions

Explain the table showing the value (in triangles) of each of the four pattern blocks shown. You may want to review the "Trading Triangles" activity. Ask the students to use the table to estimate which of the figures can be covered with exactly 10 triangles. You can have them record their guesses. Then ask them to cover each figure with the fewest pieces possible and to trace each block. Finally, have them find each block's equivalent in triangles and determine the total number of triangles within each figure. They can check this by covering the figures with triangles only.

Guided Learning

1. What strategy did you use in estimating?
2. What strategy did you use in finding the fewest number of blocks to cover a design?
3. How many triangles cover the rhombus? Hexagon? Trapezoid?

Explore More with PB!

Have students work in pairs, each making his own design and asking the partner to guess if its value is greater than, less than or equal to 10 triangles.

Building to 10

Name: _____

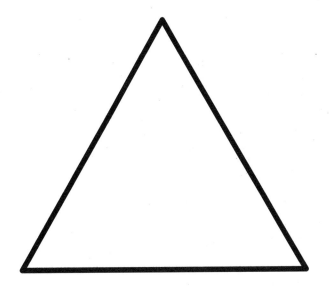

10?   yes _____ no _____

VALUE CHART
⬡ = 6
⬓ = 3
▱ = 2
△ = 1

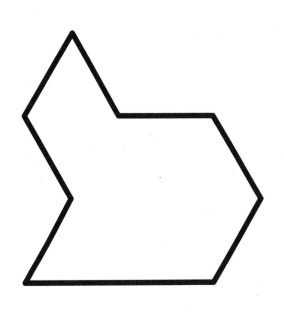

10?   yes _____ no _____

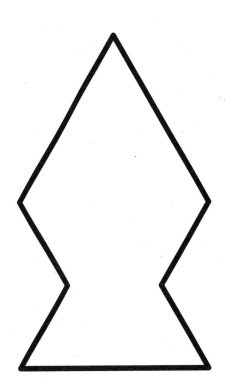

10?   yes _____ no _____

Focal Point

Number and Operations; Algebra – Using a table to describe and extend numeric (+, -) patterns.

Use physical objects to model problems. Analyze problems by observing patterns.

Materials

- Pattern blocks

Instructions

Have students build "Flower Pots" according to the pattern and then fill in the table showing the correct number in the triangles column. They should do the same with the sailboat.

Guided Learning

1. What was your strategy for filling in the table?
2. Did you need to physically make all the flowerpots and sailboats?

Explore More with PB!

Discuss the pattern. If appropriate, have the student predict how many triangles would be needed to make 6 though 10 flowerpots. Construct them and compare the guesses.

Flower Pots and Sail Boats

Name: _____

1	3
2	6
3	
4	
5	

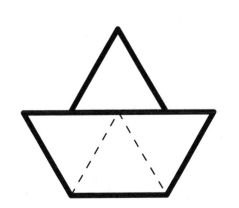 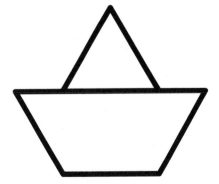

1	4
2	8
3	
4	
5	

Focal Point

Number and Operations; Algebra – Using a table to describe and extend numeric (+, -) patterns.

Use physical objects to model problems. Analyze problems by observing patterns.

Materials

- Pattern blocks

Instructions/Guided Learning

Have students use blue rhombuses to form mask A.

1. How many rhombuses would it take to make 2 masks that look exactly like this? 3? 4? 5?

Now ask them to make 5 masks and count the rhombuses necessary.

2. Were you correct?
3. In the chart, record the number of rhombuses you need for 2, 3, 4 and 5 masks.

Have them repeat activity for mask B using both rhombuses and triangles.

4. What strategy did you use to estimate your answer?

Explore More with PB!

Discuss the patterns. What if there were only triangles? How many triangles would it take to make each of the masks in the activity? Add another column to the table and record answers for triangles only. Working in pairs, have students design another mask and complete a table to accompany it.

Making Masks

Name: _____

A.

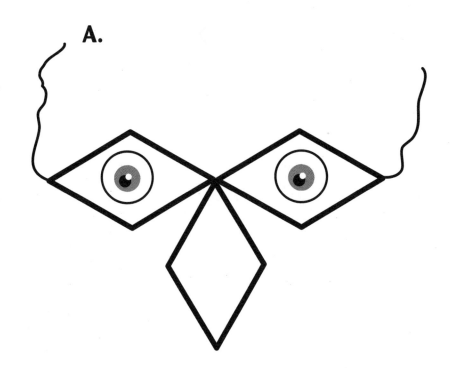

MASKS	
1	3
2	
3	
4	
5	

B.

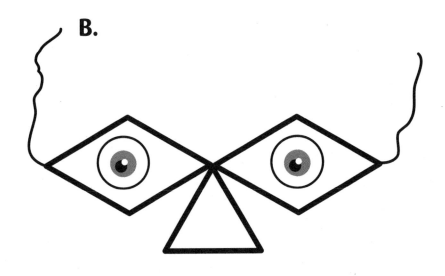

MASKS	▱	△
1	2	1
2		
3		
4		
5		

Number & Operations: **Feeding Time**

Focal Point

Number and Operations; Problem Solving – Interpreting information correctly, identifying the problem and generate possible solutions.

Use informal counting strategies to find solutions. Use a variety of strategies to compose and decompose one-digit numbers.

Materials

• 15 triangles

Instructions

Ask the students to count 15 triangles and place a different number of triangles (1, 2, 3, 4 or 5) in each bowl. Follow the path from the bowls to the animal and make sure each animal gets 6 (treats) triangles.

Guided Learning

1. Is there a different number of treats (triangles) in each bowl?

2. How many triangles does the dog have? How many triangles does the cat have? How many triangles does the duck have?

3. How did you place the triangles so that each animal received the same amount (6 triangles)?

Answers

6 Triangles:

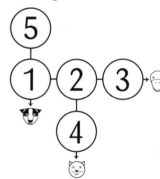

7 Triangles:

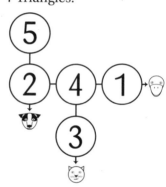

Explore More with PB!
Have students try to give each animal only 7 triangles.

Feeding Time

Name: _____

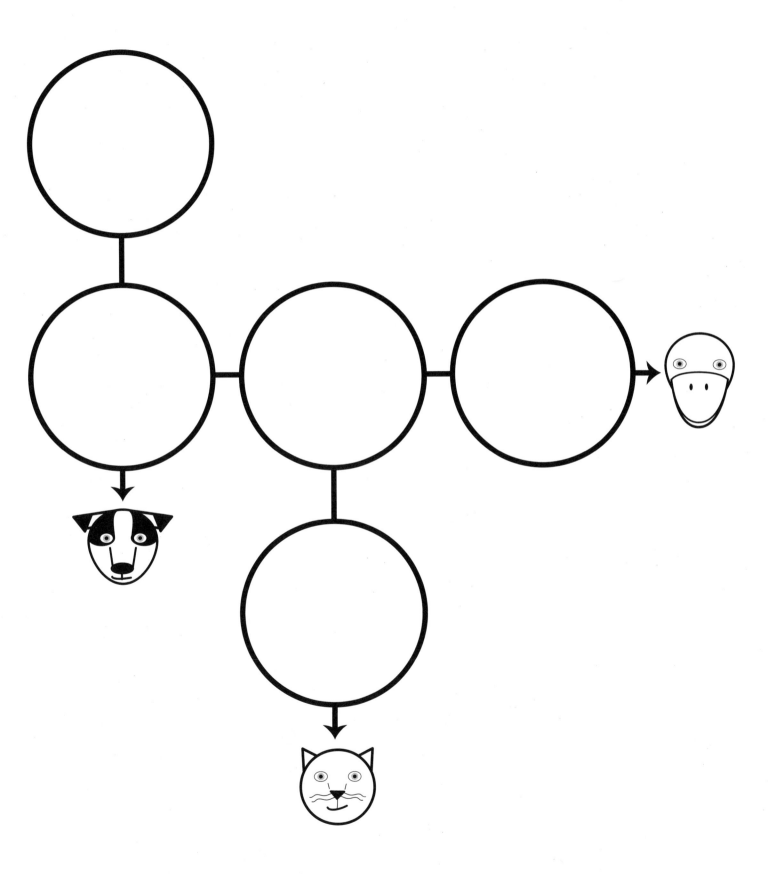

Pattern Block Book

Geometry

Geometry: **Ladybug Lane**

Focal Point

Geometry – Describing shapes and space.

Identify angles as corners of a polygon. Identify sides of a polygon. Sort shapes according to the number of angles and sides.

Materials

• Pattern blocks

Instructions

Show students the sides and the corners, using a square pattern block as an example. Show students the path the ladybug would take around the square. When she gets to the end of a SIDE, she has to make a turn. She turns at a CORNER. Ask the children to take each block and use a finger to trace the ladybug's path along the edge of the shape. For each pattern block have them count the number of sides and put the number in the correct space. Then tell them to count the number of turns the ladybug makes (corners) and put the number in the correct space.

Explore More with PB!

Students take one of each pattern block (all 6) and sort pattern blocks according to the number of sides. Next they should take an identical set of 6 pattern blocks and sort them according to the number of corners. Are the two sets of pattern blocks the same? Why? Ask if shapes made with straight sides always have the same number of sides as they have corners.

Name: _____

SQUARE

Sides? _____
Corners? _____

TRIANGLE

Sides? _____
Corners? _____

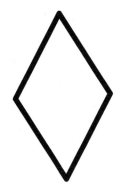

RHOMBUS

Sides? _____
Corners? _____

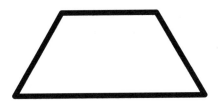

TRAPEZOID

Sides? _____
Corners? _____

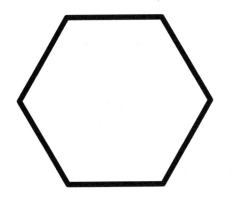

HEXAGON

Sides? _____
Corners? _____

Geometry: **Transformers**

Focal Point

Geometry – Composing and decomposing geometric shapes.

Distinguish between points on the inside (interior) and outside (exterior) of a geometric shape. Reinforce the concept of angles (corners) and count the number of angles and sides in each figure. Predict what is needed and verify the prediction, recognizing that mathematical ideas need to be supported by evidence. Explore guesses, using manipulative materials.

Materials

- Pattern blocks

Instructions/Guided Learning

Ask the students to take a yellow hexagon and place it on the worksheet, and then use a crayon to trace around the hexagon, paying attention to the sides and corners. Next, tell them to place an "x" on each side and a circle (dot) on each corner.

1. How many corners are there? How many sides are there?

Have students make another hexagon with one trapezoid, one blue rhombus and one triangle as shown on the worksheet. Using a crayon they can now trace around the outside of the hexagon, paying attention to the sides and the corners. Ask them to distinguish between the inside and the outside of the figure. Tell them again to place an "x" on each side and a circle (dot) on each corner.

2. Notice that the three blocks cover the inside of the hexagon.

3. How many corners are there? How many sides are there?

4. Do you see that the number of sides and corners stayed the same?

5. The four designs below the line are made with the same three pattern blocks you just used to make the hexagon. Look at the figures carefully.

6. Just like the with the ladybugs, each new turn indicates a new corner.

7. Will the new figures made with the same three pattern blocks have 6 sides and 6 corners?

Ask the students to move the blocks to each design and then use a crayon to trace around the outside of each figure. Then they can place an "x" on each side and a circle (dot) on each corner. Ask them to record the number of corners and sides of each new design.

8. All figures were made with the same three pattern blocks. Do all of the designs have the same number of sides? Do they all have the same number of corners? Why or why not?

Explore More with PB!

Ask children to build a new shape with 4 pattern blocks and trace the outside of the new design. They can then remove the blocks. Ask them: how many sides? How many corners? Tell them to make a shape with 5 sides and then with 6 sides.

Ask: How many corners are in each new design?

Name: _____

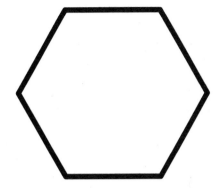

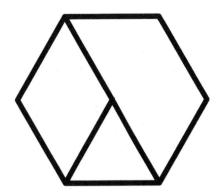

Sides? _____
Corners? _____

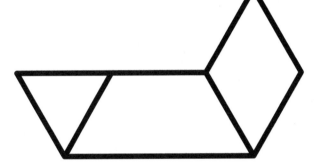

Sides? _____
Corners? _____

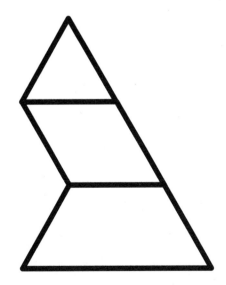

Sides? _____
Corners? _____

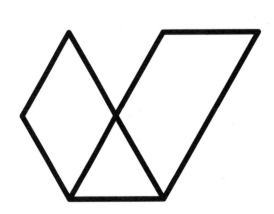

Sides? _____
Corners? _____

Geometry: **Building Squares**

Focal Point

Geometry – Describing and analyzing properties of two-dimensional shapes.

Reinforce properties and characteristics of a square. Construct and extend numeric and/or geometric patterns. Reinforce counting sets of objects greater than one and less than 20.

Materials

- 16 squares

Instructions

Students will work in pairs or in groups of three or four. Students are constructing square numbers by using blocks to build larger and larger squares.

Tell the students that squares have four sides of equal length and four corners. Build a square that has a side of two orange blocks on the overhead or draw it on the board.

Ask students to count the number of blocks in the new square and then record the number in a space on their worksheet. Now have them build a square with a side of three orange blocks and trace around the outside, recording the total number of blocks needed. Finally, have them build a square with a side of four orange blocks and trace around the outside, once again recording the total number of blocks needed.

Guided Learning

1. How many blocks are on each side of each figure?
2. How many blocks are needed to complete each figure?

Explore More with PB!

Ask students to work in groups and make a square with a side of 4 blocks. Ask them how many orange blocks are needed. How many orange blocks are on each side? Challenge question: Is there any relationship between the number of blocks on a side and the total number of blocks needed for each figure?

Building Squares

Name: _____

HOW MANY SQUARES?

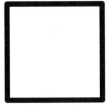

1
___

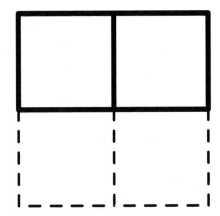

___

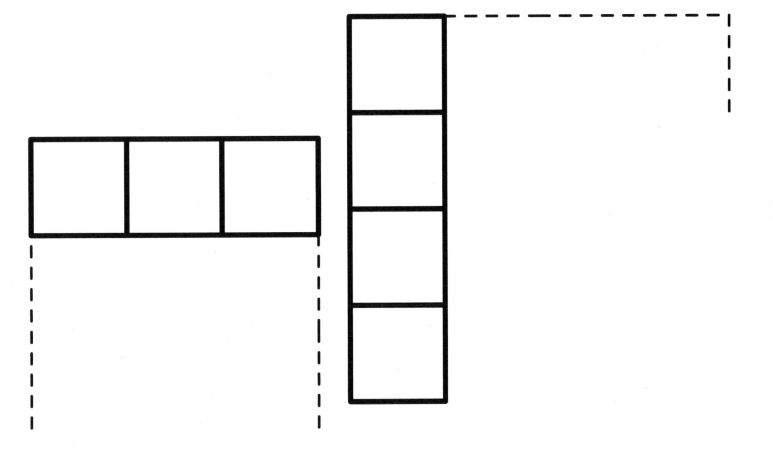

___   ___

Geometry: **Folding Figures**

Focal Point

Geometry – Describing and analyzing properties of two-dimensional shapes.

Identify geometric shapes. Introduce concept of symmetry.

Materials

- Pattern blocks
- Crayons in the colors of the pattern blocks
- Scissors

Instructions/Guided Learning

Students work in pairs. Ask them to place pattern blocks on all the figures on the page.

1. Which pattern blocks did you use for each figure?
2. How many pattern blocks did you need for each figure? How many pattern blocks did you need altogether?

Tell the students to remove the pattern blocks and color each figure the same color as the blocks. Then they should cut out each figure on the solid lines, folding it on the dotted line with the color on the outside.

3. Which folded figures look like only one pattern block?

Explore More with PB!

Ask the students to take any two of the same blocks and make a new figure, drawing a dotted line on the fold. They should color the figure the same as the blocks. Then, they should cut it out and fold it on the dotted line so color appears on both sides. Does the folded figure now look like only one pattern block?

Folding Figures

Name: _____

CUT OUT FIGURES.

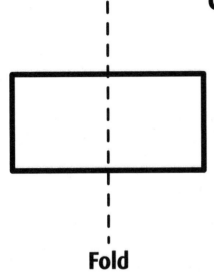

Fold

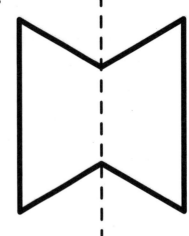

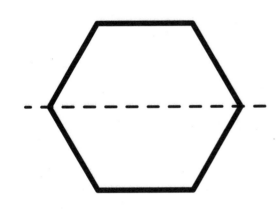

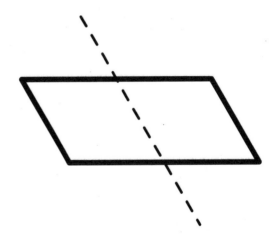

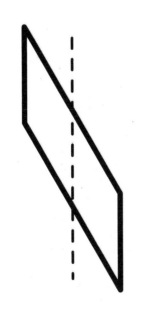

Geometry: **Folded Figures**

Focal Point

Geometry – Describing and analyzing properties of two-dimensional shapes.

Identify geometric shapes. Introduce concept of symmetry.

Materials

- Pattern blocks

Instructions

Students work in pairs. Tell them to duplicate the figure on the other side of the line and then trace around it.

Guided Learning

The figures are the same on both sides of the line but they have been folded in the middle. When the folded sides match exactly, the figures are symmetric about the line.

Explore More with PB!

(Use the reproducible giant pattern block templates on page 133.)

Ask: Which of the pattern block pieces could you fold so they are exactly the same on both sides? [Of course, they won't fold, but a picture of them will.]

Tell: Use a template of each pattern block piece. Cut it out and fold it. Draw a line to show where you folded it. Compare your folded shape with a partner

Ask: Do your folded shapes match? How are they the same? How are they different? Compare with others in the class. What do you notice?

Name: _____

OUTLINE THE SHAPE.

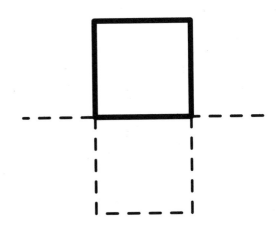

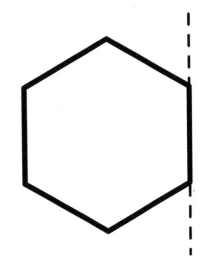

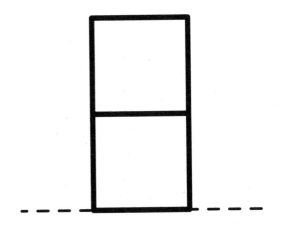

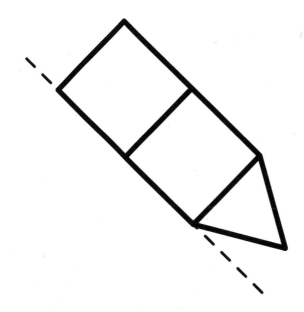

Geometry: **Butterfly Wings**

Focal Point

Geometry – Describing and analyzing properties of two-dimensional shapes.

Identify geometric shapes. Explore line of symmetry.

Materials

- Pattern blocks
- Construction paper

Instructions/Guided Learning

Students will practice reflecting shapes about a line of symmetry. Introduce these words as appropriate. Ask students to cover the first design (left side) with pattern blocks. Then have them finish the butterfly by copying the design of the blocks on the other side of the dotted line. Do the same and complete the other butterflies. You may need to demonstrate.

Explore More with PB!

Have students fold a piece of construction paper in half. Then tell them to use 4 pattern blocks to create 1 half of a new butterfly, using the fold of the paper as the line of symmetry. They should trace this and then cut out the figure. Then ask them to unfold the butterfly and decorate it.

Butterfly Wings

Name: _____

OUTLINE THE BUTTERFLY.

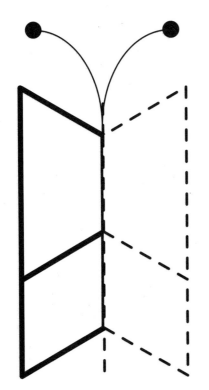

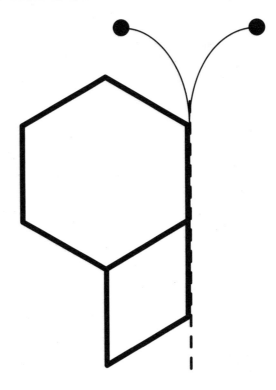

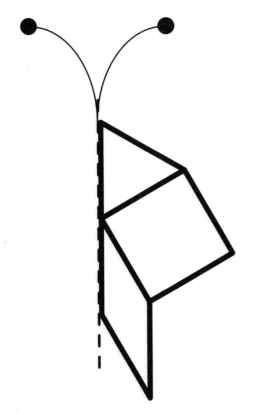

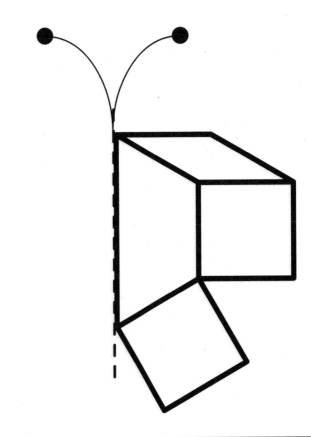

Geometry: **Growing Up**

Focal Point

Geometry – Describing and analyzing properties of two-dimensional shapes.

Measurement – Developing an understanding of area and determining the areas of two-dimensional shapes.

Materials

• Pattern blocks

Instructions/Guided Learning

Tell the students to place a triangle block on the worksheet inside the solid line. Using more triangles, add to the figure to make the next largest triangle possible with pattern blocks. Trace around the additional triangles to show the completed figure.

1. How does the new triangle compare to the original one? How much bigger is the new triangle than the original?

Ask the students to do the same thing with the rhombus, square and hexagon.

2. How does the new rhombus compare to the original one? How much bigger is the new rhombus than the original?

3. How does the new square compare to the original one? How much bigger is the new square than the original?

4. Which of the figures cannot be formed by adding blocks of the same shape?

5. Why can't we make a new hexagon by adding hexagons to the original one?

Explore More with PB!

Have students use trapezoids to make the next largest trapezoid.

Ask: What did you have to do differently to construct this figure?

Turn the pieces in a different direction than the original.

Ask: How much bigger is the new trapezoid than the original one? Tell the students to compare the number of sides and corners of the larger shape to the smaller one. Introduce the word "similar" if appropriate.

Growing Up

Name: _____

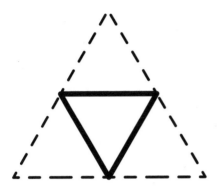

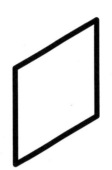

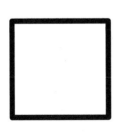

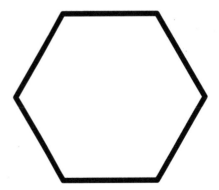

Focal Point

Geometry – Describing and analyzing properties of two-dimensional shapes.

Use manipulative materials to explore rotational symmetry.

Materials

- Pattern blocks
- Tape
- Crayons

Instructions

Have students place a square inside the solid lines in figure A. Then tell them to take a triangle and place it in position 1 on the side of the square. Now they should tape the triangle and square together using transparent or masking tape. Next, have them use a crayon to trace around the taped figure. They should then turn the figure until the square fits perfectly (position 2) and trace around the figure. They should continue this process until the figure is rotated to the start. This process will be repeated for the other figures on the worksheet.

Guided Learning

1. How many sides does the square (the starting figure) have?

2. How many different tracings did you make? How many times did you have to turn the figure to return to the starting position?

You have constructed a figure that has rotational symmetry.

3. How many sides does a triangle have? How many turns did you make to get back to the starting position?

4. Does it matter if you turned right (clockwise) or left (counterclockwise) to get back to the starting position?

Explore More with PB!

Ask the students what other pairs of pattern blocks can be used to make other figures with rotational symmetry.

Turn, Turn, Turn

Name: _____

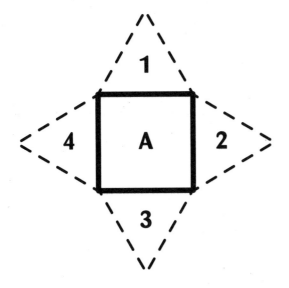

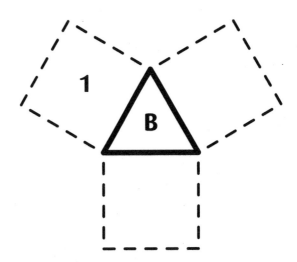

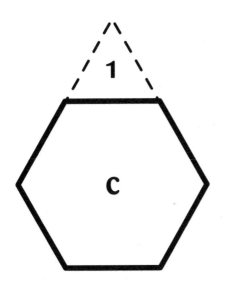

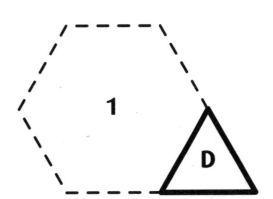

Geometry: **The Flip Side**

Focal Point

Geometry – Describing and analyzing properties of two-dimensional shapes.

Use manipulative materials to explore reflections.

Materials

- Pattern blocks
- Tape

Instructions

Ask students to build and tape the first figure. Then they should flip the taped figure across the line (reflecting it). Now have them outline the resulting figure.

Guided Learning

1. Which kind of figures were easiest to guess the result? Why?

   Students will likely mention characteristics of figures that include certain types of symmetry.

Explore More with PB!

Ask students to use 3 or 4 blocks to make a new figure and trace it.

Ask: Guess how the figure will look when you flip it (reflect it) over the dotted line. Have students sketch the guess.

Ask: Now tape the blocks together and flip (reflect) them over the dotted line. Was your guess correct? Try it again with a new figure.

Name: _____

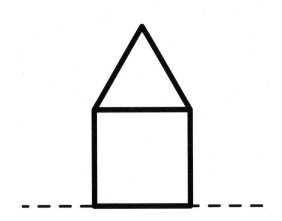

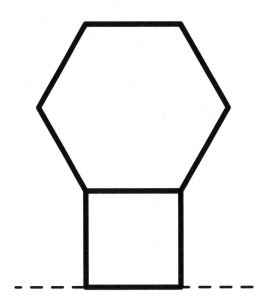

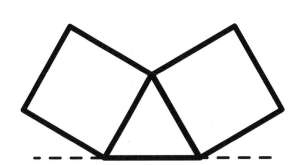

Geometry: **One Good Turn Deserves Another**

Focal Point

Geometry – Describing and analyzing properties of two-dimensional shapes.

Use manipulative materials to explore reflections and symmetry.

Materials

- Pattern blocks
- Tape

Instructions

Tell students to place blocks on figure A on the left and then tape them together. Next, they should follow the arrow and turn the figure once to position 1. Then turn again to position 2. The figure is now pointing to the right. Ask the students to look at figure B and guess how it will look in position 2 before turning it, sketching their guess. Now have them build figure B with pattern blocks taping the blocks together. They should turn the taped figure once as for figure A and draw its picture in position 1. Now they will turn the blocks to position 2.

After students complete steps 1-3, you should use the word *rotation*. We are rotating, or turning, the figure. As we do this, the figure appears to change. However, we know that the only change is in its position, nothing else changes. The figures, therefore, are said to be equivalent. They are the same figure but in a different position.

This 180 degree rotation (two 90 degree turns) about a vertical line gave the same result as a reflection. You can check this by placing a mirror on the figure on the left along the thick line with the arrow.

Explore More with PB!

Ask students to tape 3 or 4 pattern blocks together to make a new figure. Without moving the new figure, they should draw what it will look like after 2 turns. Then they can make the 2 turns with the blocks and check the result.

One Good Turn Deserves Another

Name: _____

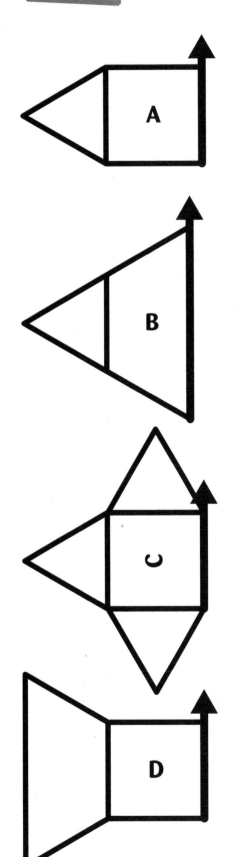

A

B

C

D

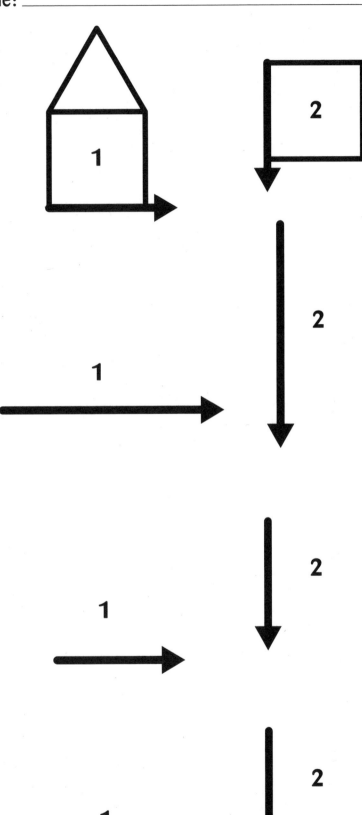

Pattern Block Book

Measurement

Measurement: **Guess and Check**

Focal Point

Geometry and Measurement – Composing and decomposing two-dimensional shapes.

Students use metric knowledge and spatial reasoning to develop foundations for understanding area, fractions and proportions.

Materials

- Pattern blocks

Instructions/Guided Learning

Ask students to predict how many hexagons it will take to cover figure A. After making their estimate, have them use hexagons to confirm.

1. Was your estimate correct? Did you estimate too many hexagons or too few hexagons?

Now have them repeat the process on figure A with the other shapes shown. Discuss their estimates. Have them move on to figure B and repeat the same process with trapezoids and then triangles. Be sure and discuss the outcome of student estimates.

2. Can you cover figure B with hexagons? With blue rhombuses? Why not?

Explore More with PB!

Tell the students to take a hexagon and place trapezoids on top of it. Discuss with students that we can cover a hexagon with 2 trapezoids and we can cover a trapezoid with three triangles. Students may explore to find other ways they can cover pattern blocks.

Name: _____

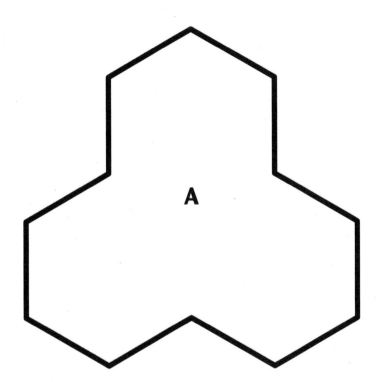

A

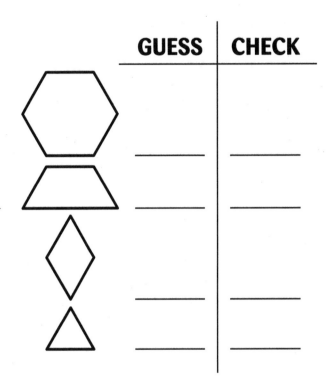

GUESS	CHECK

GUESS	CHECK

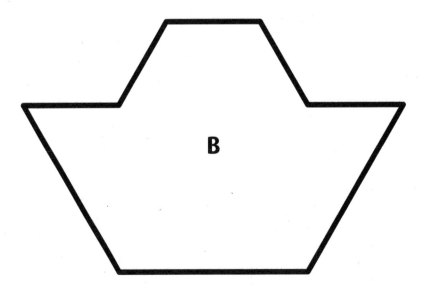

B

Measurement: **Cover All**

Focal Point

Geometry and Measurement – Using geometric knowledge and spatial reasoning to develop foundations for understanding area, fractions and proportions.

Materials

- Pattern blocks
- One-inch square grid paper (see page 132)

Instructions

Tell the students to estimate how many squares it will take to fill each figure. Then have them fill figure A. You can then discuss the concept of area with them, pointing out the number of squares they used is the area of the figure in square units. Ask them now to fill in the rest of the figures and answer the questions on the worksheet, estimating each time before using the squares.

Explore More with PB!

Working in pairs, ask the students to build a new shape with 5 square pattern blocks and then to discuss how their designs are alike and how they are different. Remind students that all their designs are equal in area. Also remind them that two designs may be identical (equivalent) even when their positions differ.

Cover All

Name: _____

A

How many ☐ ? _____

I covered the space with _____ .

The area is _____ ☐ units.

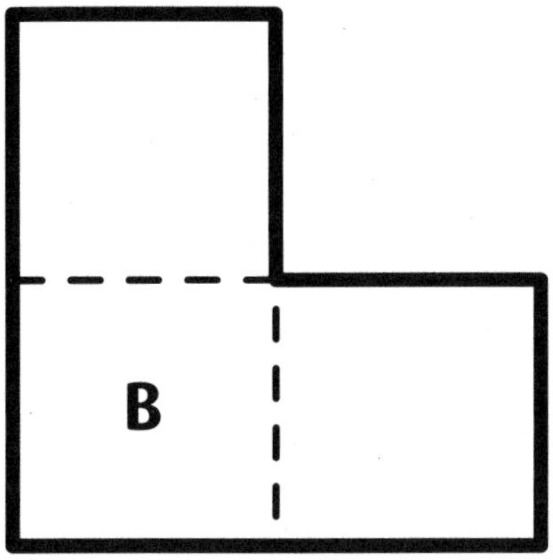

B

How many ☐ ? _____

I covered the space with _____ .

The area is _____ ☐ units.

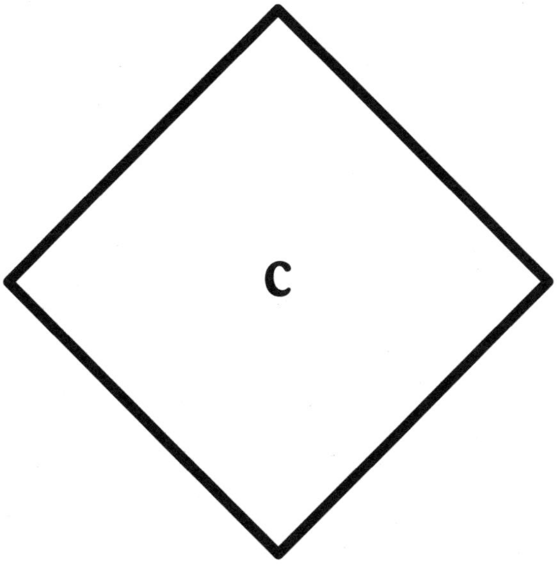

C

How many ☐ ? _____

I covered the space with _____ .

The area is _____ ☐ units.

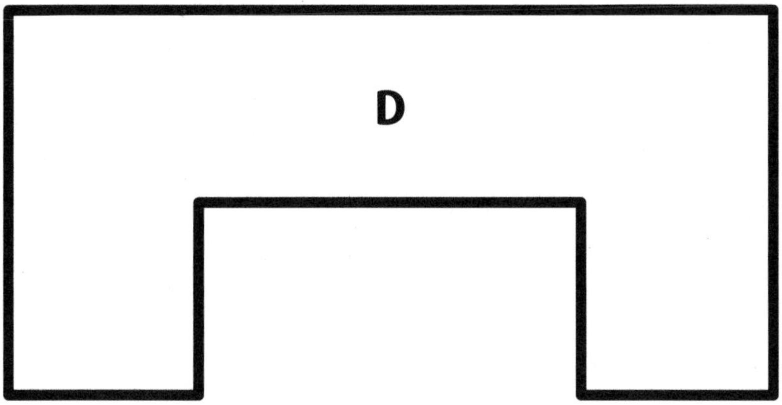

D

How many ☐ ? _____

I covered the space with _____ .

The area is _____ ☐ units.

Focal Point

Geometry and Measurement – Using geometric knowledge and spatial reasoning to develop foundations for understanding area, fractions and proportions.

Materials

• One square

Instructions

Ask students to take one square and look at it carefully. Then they should estimate the number of squares needed to cover figure A. You may want to show them how to begin measuring on an overhead projector. Tell them to use the square to trace around to show the number of squares that will be needed to fill the whole figure. They will then count and record the results. They should do this for all the figures.

Guided Learning

1. Was your guess more than, less than or the same as the actual area?

2. What did you learn about this method of measuring?

   Difficult to line up the orange square and trace around it; figure would have to be an exact number of squares or you couldn't measure it; etc.

Explore More with PB!

Have students use squared paper (page 132) to make an original design, using no more than 10 squares. Cut it out and turn it over so others cannot see the square pattern. Give it to another student to estimate and measure the area.

Cover Me, Orange!

Name: _____

A

USE ONE SQUARE. TRACE AROUND IT.

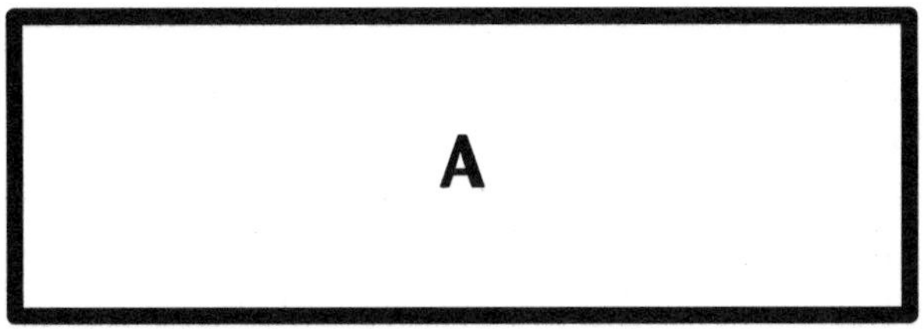

The area is _____ ☐ units.

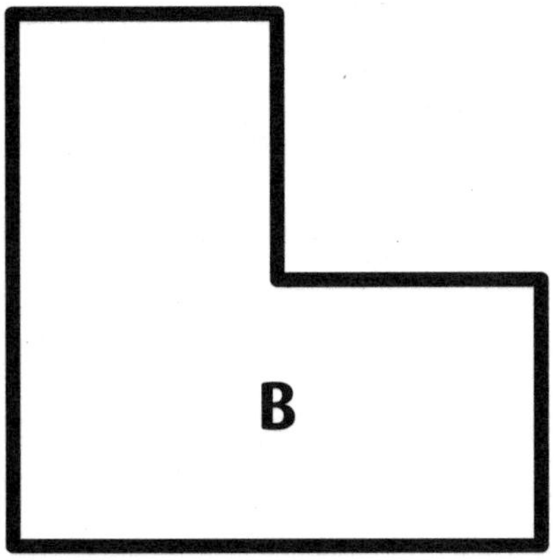

B

The area is _____ ☐ units.

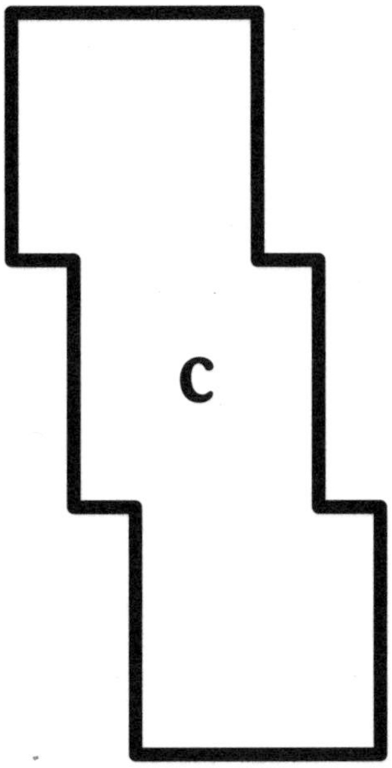

C

The area is _____ ☐ units.

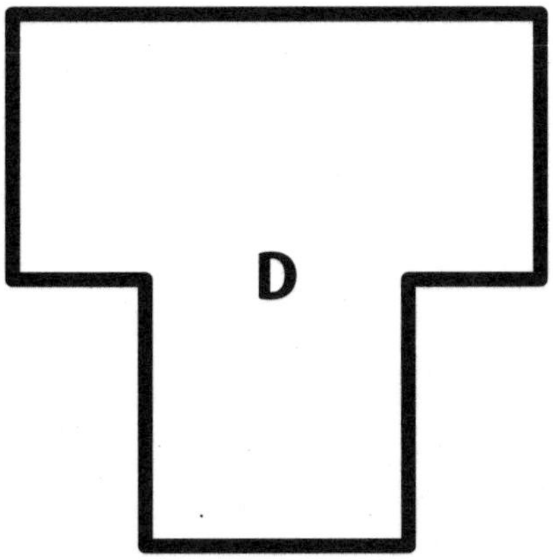

D

The area is _____ ☐ units.

Measurement: **Just One Square**

Materials

• One square

Instructions

Ask the students to estimate the number of squares needed to cover figure A and record their guesses. Using the square, students move it around inside figure A, counting how many squares would be needed to cover the figure. They will then count and enter the results next to "Area." Now, using as many squares as necessary, students cover the figure and confirm the actual area, comparing this to the number they had determined using just one square. Repeat for all figures.

Guided Learning

1. How does your "measured area" compare with the actual area?

2. What did you learn about this method of measuring?

   Difficult to move the orange square and make sure it is in the right place; figure would have to be an exact number of squares or you couldn't measure it; etc.

3. What is the order of the figures from the smallest to the largest area?

Explore More with PB!

Using squared paper (page 132), students draw and cut out 4 different shapes each using exactly 6 squares. They can then compare the shapes. Ask them if the area of these shapes are all the same or different.

Just One Square

Name: _____

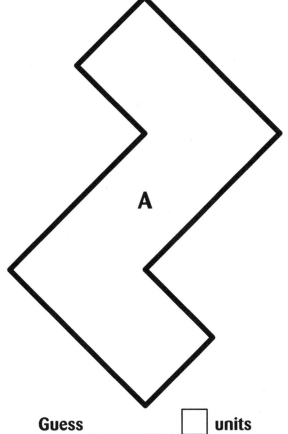

A

Guess _____ ☐ **units**

Area _____ ☐ **units**

B

Guess _____ ☐ **units**

Area _____ ☐ **units**

C

Guess _____ ☐ **units**

Area _____ ☐ **units**

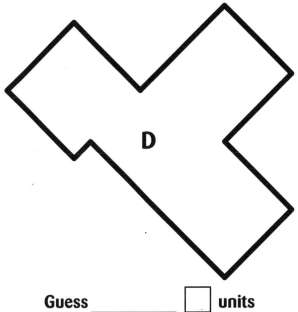

D

Guess _____ ☐ **units**

Area _____ ☐ **units**

Measurement: **Undercover**

Focal Point

Geometry and Measurement – Using geometric knowledge and spatial reasoning to develop foundations for understanding area, fractions and proportions.

Materials

- Three squares

Instructions

Working in pairs, the students first estimate the area of each shape, recording guesses. Next, partners should work together to measure the area of each shape using only three squares. Results should be recorded.

Guided Learning

1. What strategy did you use to determine the area?

Explore More with PB!

Each pair of students should design a large shape using squared paper (page 132), and then cut out the shape and turn it over to hide the lines. Another pair of students then can estimate and measure the area of the new shape. What advice would they give someone else who needs to measure something? Have them write about their shape in their math journal.

Name: _____

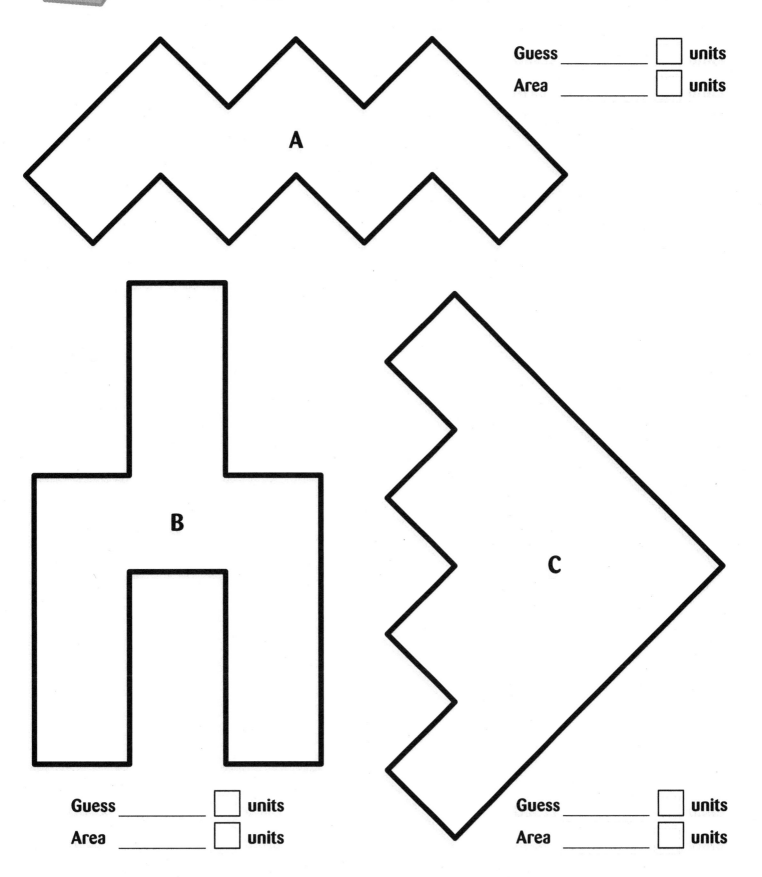

Guess _____ ☐ units
Area _____ ☐ units

A

B

C

Guess _____ ☐ units
Area _____ ☐ units

Guess _____ ☐ units
Area _____ ☐ units

Focal Point

Measurement – Forming an understanding of perimeter as a measurable attribute and selecting appropriate units, strategies and tools to solve problems involving perimeter.

Recognize length as an attribute that can be measured. Use non-standard units to measure both vertical and horizontal lengths. Informally introduce the idea of perimeter. Compare and order pattern blocks from largest to smallest perimeter.

Materials

- Orange squares
- One rhombus
- One hexagon
- One trapezoid

Instructions

1. Watch as your teacher shows you how to find the perimeter of a triangle.
2. Place orange squares around the triangle.
3. Count and record the number of squares necessary.
4. Repeat 2-3 for each remaining shape.

Instructions/Guided Learning

Using an overhead projector, take one square and place it along the side of triangle A. Compare the lengths of the side of the square to the length of the side of the triangle. Tell the students that this length is one unit. Now take two more squares so there is one square along each side of the triangle. Each time compare the length of one side of the square to the length of one side of the triangle.

Ask the students to place squares on each edge of the triangle in figure 1. Then remove the squares and write "1" on each side of the triangle as shown here:

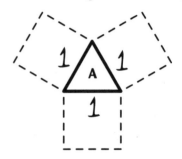

Explain that the number of units around the entire triangle is the perimeter (1 + 1 + 1 = 3). Now have the student find the perimeter of each of the remaining pattern blocks.

1. Do all these shapes have the same perimeter or different perimeters?
2. Name the pattern blocks in order from the largest to the smallest perimeter.

Explore More with PB!

Have students make a new shape using any three pattern blocks and outline it on paper. They can then find the perimeter using orange squares. Have another student estimate its perimeter and record the estimate. Have the student measure the figure and compare answers.

How Far Around?

Name: _____

 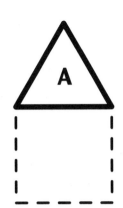 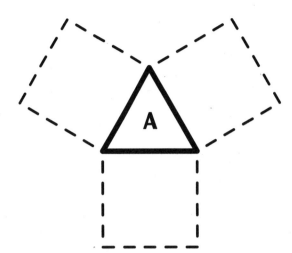

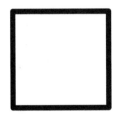

Perimeter: _____ units

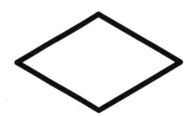

Perimeter: _____ units

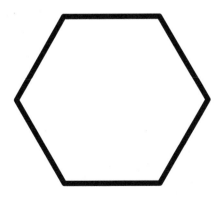

Perimeter: _____ units

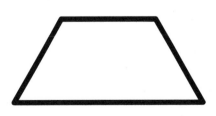

Perimeter: _____ units

Focal Point

Measurement – Forming an understanding of perimeter as a measurable attribute and selecting appropriate units, strategies and tools to solve problems involving perimeter.

Use informal counting strategies to find solutions. Continue to develop concept of perimeter. Develop the concept of using one unit repeatedly (iteration) to measure the length around an object.

Materials

- One square

Instructions

Review the concept of perimeter. Ask students to use one pattern block to determine the perimeter of figure A, recording their answers. You may need to prompt students to mark the edge of the square each time they move it. Ask them to repeat this for the other figures.

Guided Learning

1. How does the estimated perimeter of each figure compare to the measured perimeter?

2. Is the estimated perimeter greater than, less than or the same as the measured perimeter?

Explore More with PB!

After estimating, have students use the side of a square to find the perimeter of a textbook or notebook and compare other objects in the classroom. Have them record both their estimate and their measured perimeters.

Name: _____

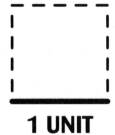

1 UNIT

USE ONE SQUARE TO MEASURE THE PERIMETER.

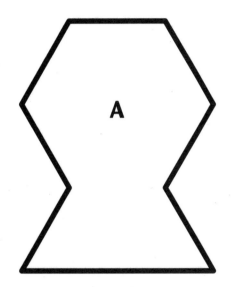

A

Perimeter: _____ units

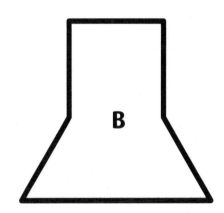

B

Perimeter: _____ units

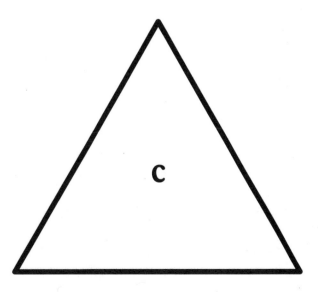

C

Perimeter: _____ units

Measurement: **Sizing Up**

Focal Point

Measurement – Forming an understanding of perimeter as a measurable attribute and selecting appropriate units, strategies and tools to solve problems involving perimeter.

Compare measurements of area and perimeter. Students make, investigate and validate mathematical conjectures.

Materials

- One square

Instructions

Ask students to find the area of each figure and record it. Discuss. Then using one square, they should find and record the perimeter of each figure.

Guided Learning

1. Why is the area the same for each figure?
2. Do you think all the perimeters will be the same? Why?
3. Do figures with the same area have the same perimeter? Is this always true?

Explore More with PB!

Ask students to make and trace figures using 5 squares, finding their areas and perimeters. Have them try to make 2 of these figures with different perimeters.

Name: _____

USE 1 ONLY

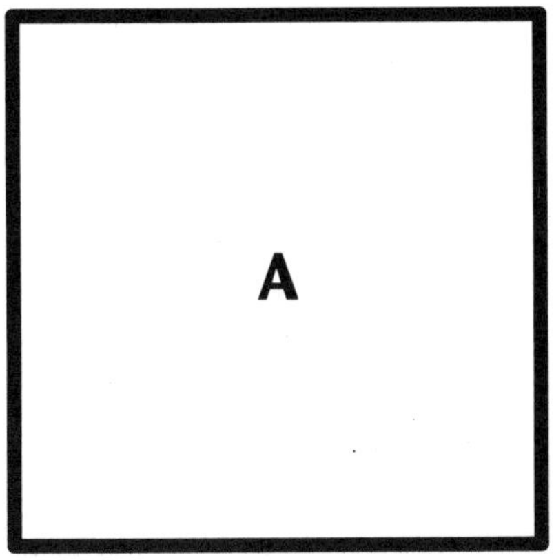

A

Area _____ ☐ units

Perimeter: _____ units

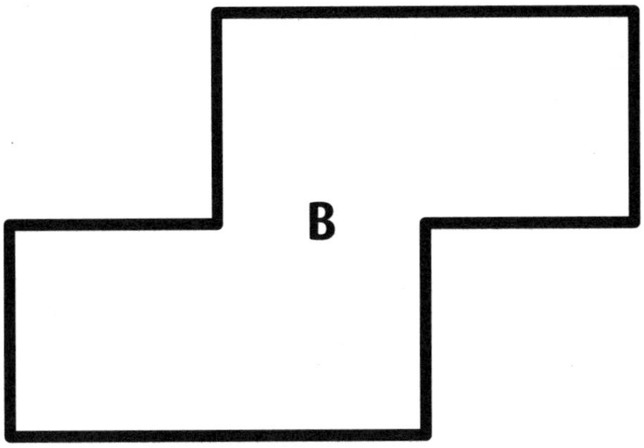

B

Area _____ ☐ units

Perimeter: _____ units

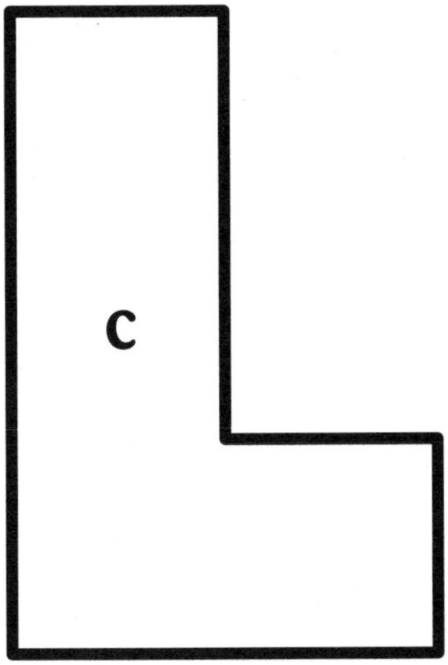

C

Area _____ ☐ units

Perimeter: _____ units

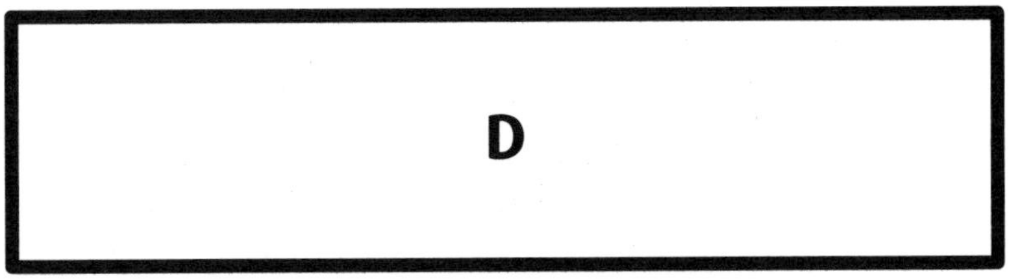

D

Area _____ ☐ units

Perimeter: _____ units

Measurement: **All the Right Angles**

Focal Point

Geometry – Describing and analyzing properties of two-dimensional shapes.

Use the concepts of measurement to identify right angles.

Materials

- Pattern blocks

Instructions/Guided Learning

Ask students to color the interior of each figure.

1. How many sides and how many corners does the square have?

Ask them to place a corner of the orange square on "1" in figure A.

2. Do they match exactly? We call corner "1" a "right angle."

3. How many right angles are in figure A?

4. How many right angles are in the small orange square?

Now tell the students to continue numbering all the angles in figure B. Using an orange square as a guide they should put a circle around the number at each right angle.

5. How many angles in figure B?

6. How many of them are right angles?

The students can now repeat the activity with figure C and D. Continue to ask them questions as before.

Explore More with PB!

Tell students to use the orange square to determine the number of angles in each pattern block.

Ask: Which pattern blocks have all right angles?

Square

Ask: Which blocks have no right angles?

All other pattern blocks

Have students use the orange square to help them identify right angles in the classroom.

All the Right Angles

Name: _____

LABEL THE ANGLES. CIRCLE THE RIGHT ANGLES.

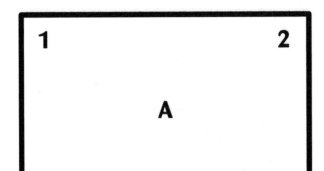

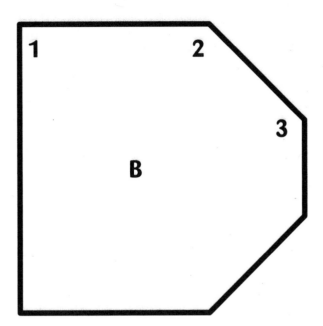

A

B

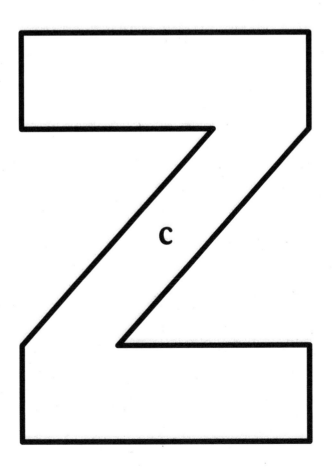

C

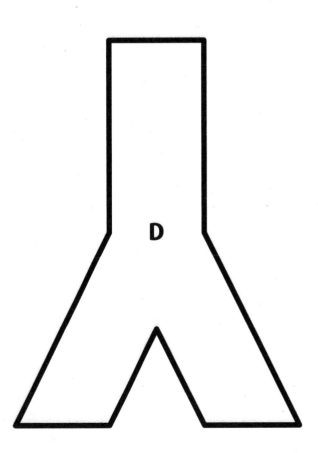

D

Measurement: **Moving Pictures**

Focal Point

Measurement – Forming an understanding of perimeter as a measurable attribute and selecting appropriate units, strategies and tools to solve problems involving perimeter.

Compare measurements of area and perimeter. Students make, investigate and validate mathematical conjectures.

Materials

- Pattern blocks

Instructions/Guided Learning

Ask students to take 6 squares and make as many different figures as possible on the grid. They should outline each figure and color it in using one color. Then they will write the number of squares on each figure.

1. How many squares did you color? This number is the area.

Ask them to outline the outside of each figure with a different color from the one on the inside. They can then write the measurement of perimeter next to each figure.

2. Are the areas the same or are they different?

3. Are the perimeters the same or are they different?

Ask the students to number the right angles in each figure.

Explore More with PB!

Repeat the process using 12 squares. This time, students should make only rectangles.

Ask: How many different rectangles can be made? Do rectangles with the same area always have the same perimeter?

Students should explain their answers.

Ask: How many angles does each rectangle have? How many right angles does each rectangle have? What can you say about the angles and the right angles?

All angles in a rectangle are also right angles.

Name: _____

Pattern Block Book

Algebra

Focal Point

Algebra – Identifying, duplicating and extending patterns and sequential and growing patterns.

Materials

- Pattern blocks

Instructions

Ask the students to put patterns blocks on the corresponding shapes on line 1. Then tell them to decide which block comes next and to put it on the dotted line. They will repeat this process with the other lines.

Guided Learning

1. Describe each pattern using the color and the shape of the pattern block in your descriptions.
2. What is the rule for each pattern?

Explore More with PB!

Ask the students to see if each pattern can be completed another way. Suggest that they build a pattern of their own. They should build and trace the first four "pictures" of the pattern. Have them ask a partner to predict what comes next. The partner can be asked to explain the rule.

Patterns

Name: _____

1. 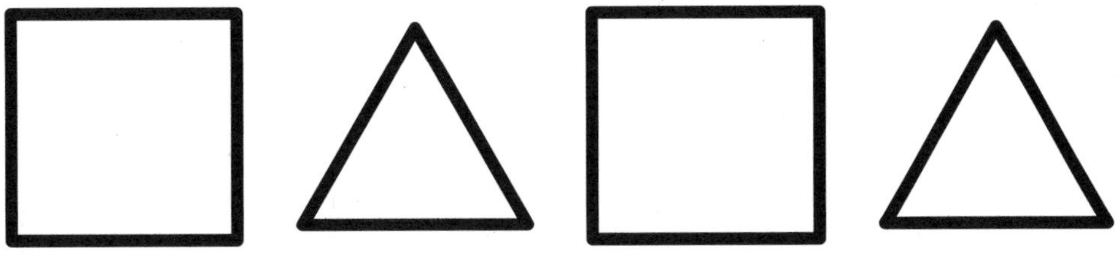 ▢ △ ▢ △ _ _ _ _ _ _ _ _

2.  ▢ ▱ ▢ ▱ _ _ _ _ _ _ _ _

3. △ ▢ ▢ △ ▢ _ _ _ _ _ _ _

4. 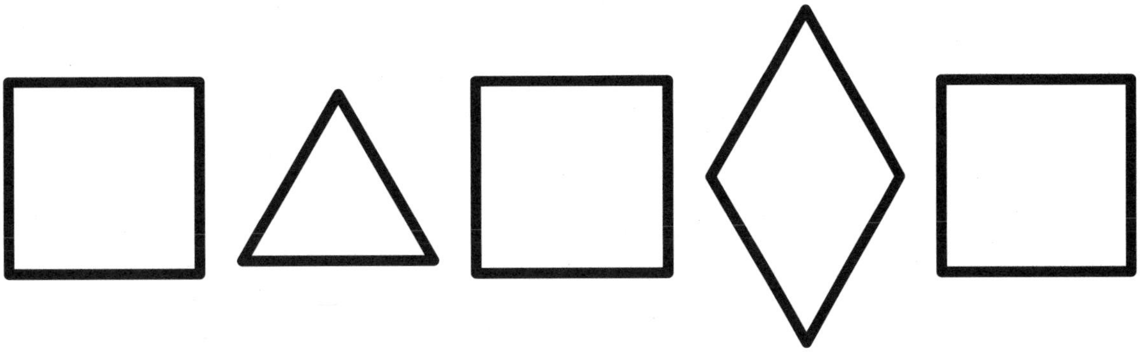 ▢ △ ▢ ◇ ▢ _ _ _ _ _ _ _

5. 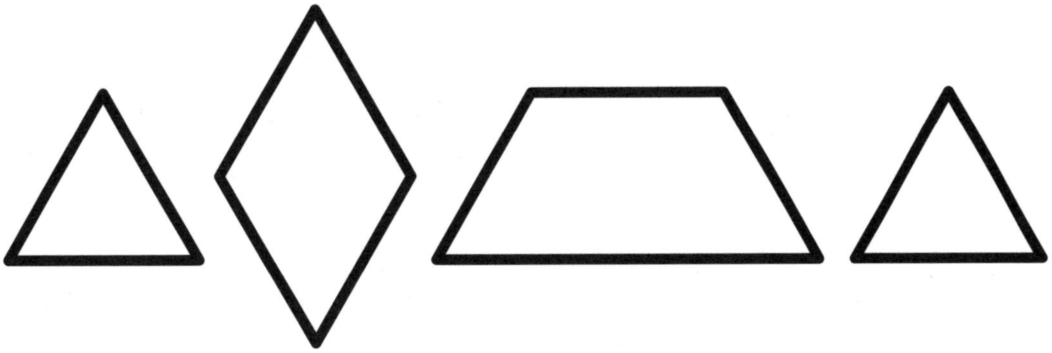 △ ◇ ⬠ △ _ _ _ _ _ _ _ _

Focal Point

Algebra – Identifying, duplicating and extending patterns and sequential and growing patterns.

Materials

- Pattern blocks

Instructions

Ask the students to set up the pattern blocks shown on line 1 on their desktops. Next, tell them to decide what the next two groups of pattern blocks will be on this line. They should build the rest of the line and explain the rule they used. Have them repeat this process for all lines.

Guided Learning

The pictures on the worksheet change according to a rule; they do not repeat themselves. Such lists of pictures are sometimes called growing patterns, but they are really sequences.

Explore More with PB!

Ask if each sequence can be completed another way. Suggest that students create a sequence of their own. They can build and trace the first 4 pictures of the sequence and then ask a partner to predict what comes next. Have them record the number of blocks needed for each picture in the sequence. Ask the students to predict how many blocks will be needed altogether for the next 3 pictures.

Name: _____

1.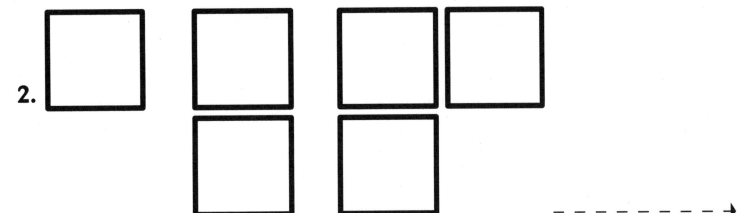

2.

3.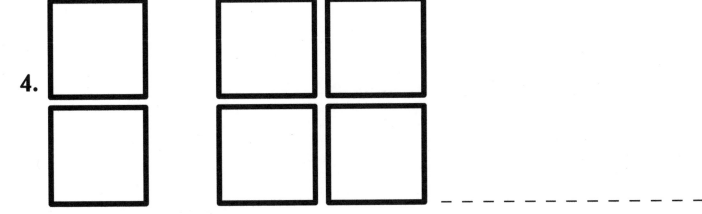

4.

Algebra: **Building Towers**

Focal Point

Algebra – Identifying, duplicating and extending patterns and sequential and growing patterns; developing rules to explain extensions.

Materials

- Pattern blocks

Instructions

Explain that each line shows a sequence. Ask students to complete the next two towers by using pattern blocks on their desks. They can then record results on the worksheet.

Guided Learning

1. Describe each sequence using the color and the shape of the pattern block in your description.

2. Keep in mind that some sequences may be able to be completed in several different ways.

3. Give the rule for your answers.

Explore More with PB!

Have students build their own towers, writing down the number of blocks needed for the first 5 towers. Ask a partner to discover the sequence. Suggest students make a 2-color tower sequence, completing the first 4 towers and showing them to a partner.

Ask: What will the next tower be?

Name: _____

1.

2.

3.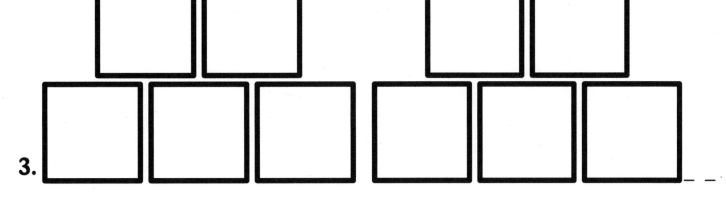

Focal Point

Algebra – Identifying, duplicating and extending patterns and sequential and growing patterns; developing rules to explain extensions.

Materials

- Pattern blocks

Instructions

Have students construct the sequences shown on their desks. They should then work out what the next 2 pictures should be, recording their answers on the dotted lines for each sequence.

Guided Learning

1. Describe each sequence using the color and the shape of the pattern block in your description.
2. Keep in mind that some sequences may be able to be completed in several different ways.
3. Give the rule for each sequence.

Explore More with PB!

Working with a partner, students find other ways to complete each sequence. Suggest they discuss their strategies for finding the rule for each sequence.

Fancy Designs

Name: _____

1.  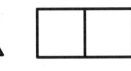 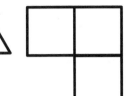 - - - - - - - - →

2.  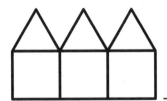   - - - - - - - - →

3.   - - - - - - - - →

4. 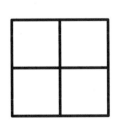 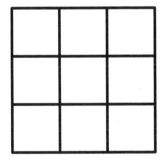 - - - - - - - - →

5.    - - - - - - - - →

Focal Point

Algebra – Using number patterns to extend their knowledge of properties of numbers and operations.

Materials

• Pattern blocks

Instructions

Tell students to put a pattern block triangle on each shaded triangle in figure A, B and C. They will see that they are adding a row of triangles each time for figures B and C. They should record the number of triangles needed below each figure.

Guided Learning

1. Just considering the numbers, determine how many triangles will be needed to complete figure D to have it follow the previous sequence. Record your estimate.

2. Build figure D, adding triangles to make picture D similar to A, B and C. Altogether, how many triangles did you need? Was your estimate correct?

3. Did you use a strategy? Explain it.

Explore More with PB!

Ask: If the total number of shaded triangles in towers A through D is 1, 3, 6, 10, ... , how many triangles would you need for tower E? Why?

Have students repeat this activity filling in all of the triangles (shaded or not). Tell them to record the results and compare the two sequences. Compare 1, 3, 6, 10, ...to 1, 4, 9, 16, ...

Triangle Towers

Name: _____

A.

1
_____

B.

_____

C.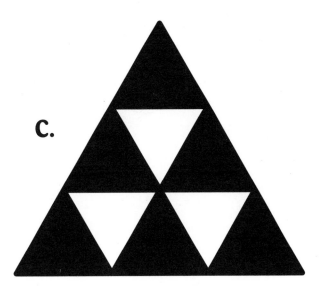

_____

D.

_____

Algebra: **Seesaws**

Focal Point

Algebra – Using patterns, models and relationships as contexts for writing and solving simple equations and inequalities.

Materials

- Pattern blocks

Instructions/Guided Learning

Ask the students to hold their arms straight outward (parallel to the floor) and tilt them like a seesaw imagining that they have a heavy weight in their left hand (right arm up, left arm down) or in their right hand (left arm up, right arm down). Tell them to take the 2 pattern blocks that are shown at figure A and put them on the outlines on the seesaw.

1. Why is the way the pattern blocks are on the seesaw correct?

2. What would happen to the seesaw if the blocks were switched?

Ask students to place the other pattern blocks on the seesaws B, C and D to show the best arrangement. Tell them to trace the pattern blocks on the seesaw.

3. Why did you put the pattern blocks where you did?

Explore More with PB!

Ask students to select 2 other pattern blocks. Ask them to draw how the seesaw would look. Have them trace and color their pattern blocks at each end of the seesaw.

Name: _____

A.

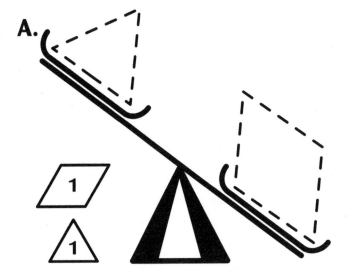

B.

C.

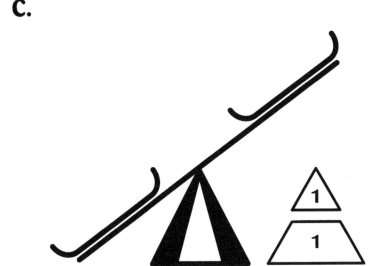

D.

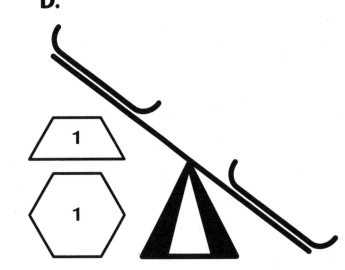

- -

YOUR SEESAW

Focal Point

Algebra – Using patterns, models and relationships as contexts for writing and solving simple equations and inequalities.

Introduce symbols =, < and > to show the relationships among indicated blocks. Use knowledgeable guessing as a mathematical tool.

Materials

• Pattern blocks

Instructions/Guided Learning

Ask the students to look at figure A and to place the pieces on each side of the seesaw as shown. Ask them to explain why this is the correct placement. Discuss what would happen to the seesaw if the pattern blocks were switched. Now ask the students to place the other pattern blocks on seesaws B, C and D. They should trace each pattern block. Discuss why these are correct placements.

1. Could they have been placed differently and still be correct?

2. How many different ways are there to place them for seesaws A, B, C and D?

Explore More with PB!

Ask students to select any 3 of the following pattern blocks (triangle, trapezoid, hexagon, blue rhombus) and determine an arrangement for a seesaw. Ask them to draw the seesaw with the blocks on it on a piece of paper. On the fulcrum (center) of the seesaw, students should put a less than, greater than or equal sign to show the relationship between the blocks on the left side of the seesaw and the right side of the seesaw, in terms of "weight" (not the number of pieces). Ask them to think of another arrangement with the same 3 blocks and draw its picture. Again, they should put < , > or = to indicate the appropriate relationship.

Name: _____

A.

B.

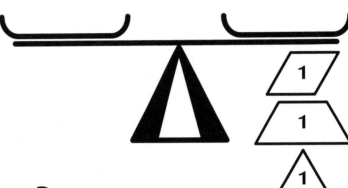

C.

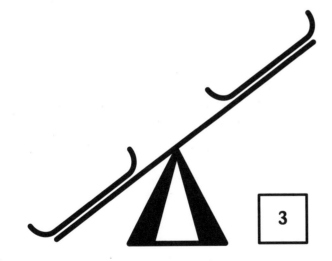

D.

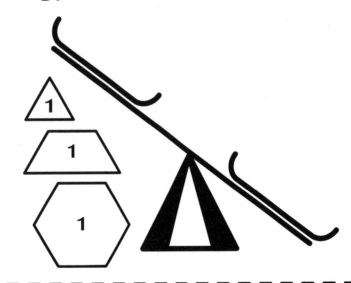

- -

YOUR SEESAW

Algebra: **Missing Pieces**

Focal Point

Algebra and Geometry – Composing and decomposing two-dimensional shapes.

Recognize a geometric shape as missing after placement of given pattern blocks.

Materials

- Pattern blocks

Instructions/Guided Learning

Ask students to look at figure A. Tell them to take the number of patterns blocks shown and place them on figure A.

1. What piece is missing?
   Triangle
2. How did you figure this out?

Tell them to repeat with the other figures on the page.

Explore More with PB!

Ask the student to look at figures A, B and C only. Tell them to place 3 triangles to cover part of each shape and trace and color them.

Ask: How much is missing? Give your answer in triangles.

Missing Pieces

Name: _____

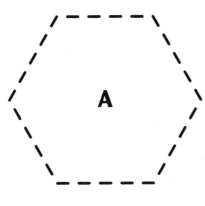

A

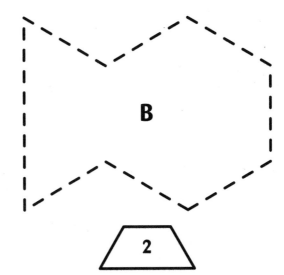

B

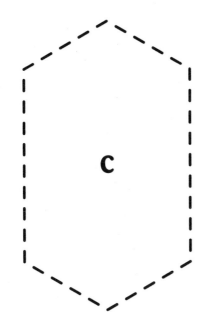

C

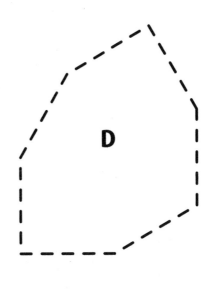

D

Focal Point

Algebra – Using patterns, models and relationships as contexts for writing and solving simple equations and inequalities.

Materials

- Pattern blocks

Instructions

Have students look at the seesaw. Point out that neither side of the seesaw is up or down. Therefore, the seesaw is balanced. The same amount (of weight) is on each end.

Ask student to take the blocks shown for seesaw A and place them so that the left side equals the right side, tracing their results. Tell them to put an equal sign over the fulcrum. They should repeat for all figures.

Guided Learning

1. How do you know the sides are equal?
2. What symbols would you use over the fulcrum if it were not balanced?

   $<, >$
3. Be able to explain how you know that the two sides are equal.
4. Put the equals sign on the fulcrum.
5. Repeat steps 2-4 for seesaws B, C and D.

Explore More with PB!

Ask students to take any 6 pieces and place them on your seesaw so that the seesaw is balanced (the weight is the same on each side). Then they should trace the pieces, putting an = sign on the fulcrum. Ask that they explain how they know the seesaw is balanced.

Balance the Seesaw

Name: _____

A. TAKE

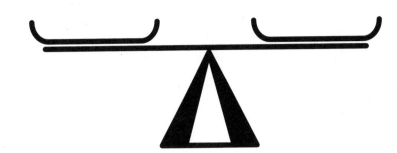

B. TAKE

C. TAKE

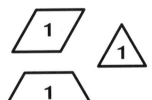

D. TAKE

Focal Point

Algebra – Using, organizing and representing patterns and functions.

Materials

- Pattern blocks

Instructions

Explain that each robot has a different rule for what goes in and what comes out. By looking closely at lines A and B, students should be able to guess the rule and complete line C.

Guided Learning

1. A robot is changing the number of pattern blocks. Sometimes it adds blocks and sometimes it takes them away. The robot is following a secret rule.

2. Look at line A. How many triangles go into machine 1? How many triangles come out?

3. What happens on line B?

   2 go in; 4 come out

   Since the machine is doing the same thing, if 3 triangles go into the machine on line C, how many come out? What is the rule?

   Double the number of blocks

4. Look at machine 2. On your desk, use pattern blocks to show lines A, B and C of machine 2. In line C, which pattern blocks will come out of machine 2? Explain what has happened. Write the robot's secret rule for machine 2.

5. Do the same for machines 3 and 4.

Explore More with PB!

Ask students to look at the machine 4 and complete the table below, filling in the blanks

	IN	OUT
Line A	8	4
Line B	4	___
Line C	___	___

Name: _____

1. IN  OUT

A.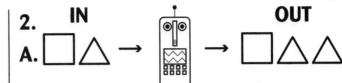

B.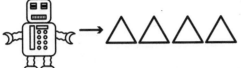

2. IN OUT

C.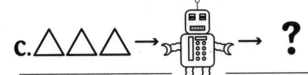

IN   OUT

3.

A.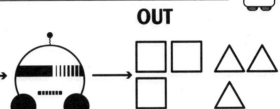

B.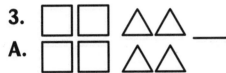

C.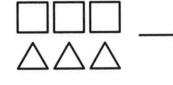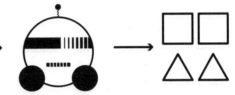

4.

A.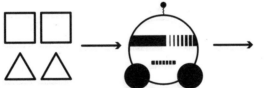

B.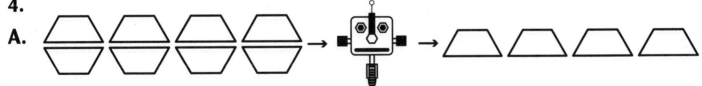

C.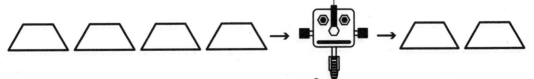

Pattern Block Book

Probability & Statistics

Focal Point

Data Analysis – Representing measurements and discrete data in picture and bar graphs.

Materials

- Pattern blocks

Instructions

Part 1 (Worksheet 1)

Tell students to choose the necessary pattern blocks and use them to make the picture of the person flying a kite. Then tell them to remove all the blocks and group them according to color, counting the number of blocks of each kind and recording in the table.

Part 2 (Worksheet 2)

Show them how to graph the results by coloring one square in the graph for each block.

Explore More with PB!

Ask students to create their own picture with various pattern blocks. Then have them record in the table and bar graph on worksheet 2.

Flying a Kite (1)

Name: _____

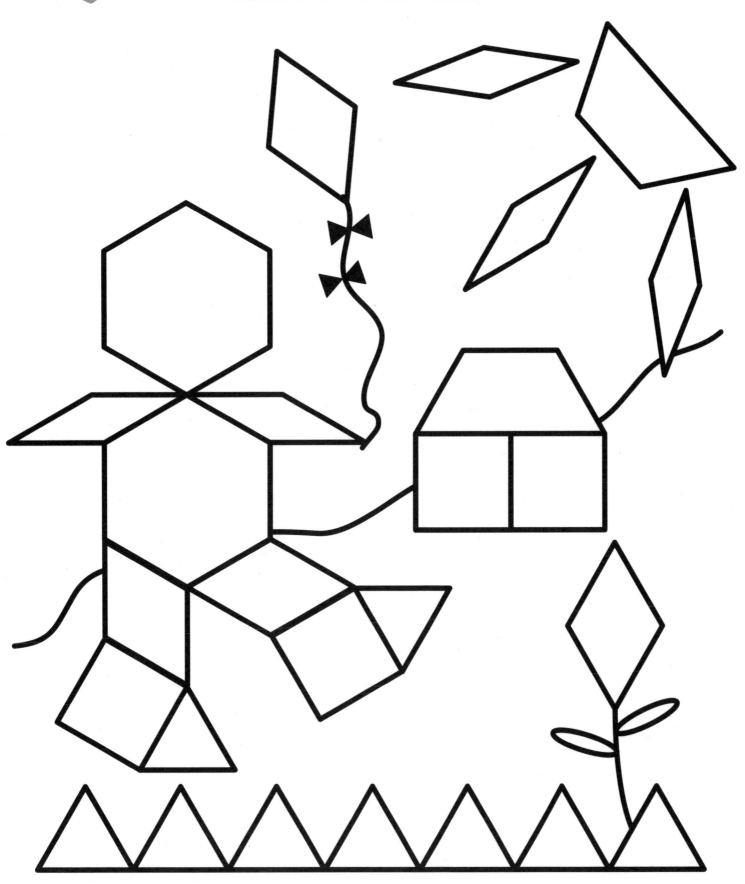

Name: _____

I Used

_____ 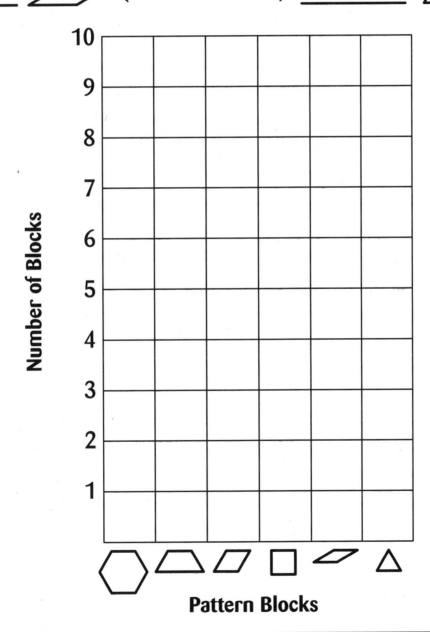 (hexagons)   _____ (trapezoids)

_____ (blue rhombuses)   _____ (squares)

_____ (tan rhombuses)   _____ (triangles)

Number of Blocks

10
9
8
7
6
5
4
3
2
1

Pattern Blocks

Probability & Statistics: Quite a Handful

Focal Point

Data Analysis – Constructing and analyzing frequency tables, bar graphs, picture graphs and line plots and use them to solve problems.

Construct a frequency table to represent a collection of data.

Materials

- A large group of pattern blocks
- A bucket or bag
- One worksheet per student

Instructions

Students work in pairs.

Part 1 (Worksheet 1)

Have student 1 take a handful of pattern blocks from the bucket (bag). The pattern blocks are to be sorted according to color and shape. Have him record the number in the table provided below under Handful A. Next, student 1 takes another handful and does the same, recording under Handful B. Tell the student to put both handfuls together, sort them and record the total number in the column marked total. [Students may add or count to get this information.] Now ask student 2 to repeat this and record on her worksheet.

Part 2 (Worksheet 2)

Cut the worksheet in half and provide to the appropriate students. Ask the students to graph their TOTAL results from worksheet 1. Then the students should compare their graphs.

Guided Learning

1. How are the graphs alike? How are they different?
2. Did you have the same total number of blocks for Handfuls A and B? Which handful was bigger?
3. Which pattern block did you have the most of? Was that the same for your partner?
4. Which pattern block did you have the least of? Was that the same for your partner?
5. How many pattern blocks altogether did you and your partner pick up?

Explore More with PB!

Have students redo the activity again, estimating the number of each kind of block they will grab. They should count and graph their results. Ask them to compare with their partner and discuss the results.

Quite a Handful (1)

Name: _____

A.   **B.**

	Handful A	Handful B	Total
⬡			
⬠			
▱			
△			
▢			
▱			

Quite a Handful (2)

Name: _____

Total Blocks Student 1

Total Blocks Student 2

15
14
13
12
11
10
9
8
7
6
5
4
3
2
1

15
14
13
12
11
10
9
8
7
6
5
4
3
2
1

Focal Point

Data Analysis – Constructing and analyzing frequency tables, bar graphs, picture graphs and line plots and use them to solve problems.

Construct a frequency table to represent a collection of data. Use data to make predictions.

Materials

- A large group of pattern blocks
- A bucket or bag

Instructions

Students work in pairs.

Ask student 1 to take a handful of pattern blocks from the bucket (bag) without looking. Any blocks that fall are returned to the bucket and do not count. Pattern blocks should be sorted according to color and shape and results recorded in the table provided under Handful A. Tell students to keep each handful they grab and put it aside. Now student 2 takes another handful and repeats the above, recording under Handful B. Next, student 1 takes blocks and records the results in the table for Handful C.

Ask both students to look at the table and try to estimate how many blocks will be chosen in total for Handful D, recording their estimate on the dotted line. Finally have student 2 take blocks and record in the table for Handful D.

Guided Learning

1. What information did you use to make your estimate?
2. Was your estimate for Handful D greater or less than the actual count?
3. What is the difference between your estimate and Handful D?

Explore More with PB!

Ask students to review the count in Handfuls A, B, C and D. Are all handfuls the same in number? Now ask them to move the pattern blocks from one handful to another so that all handfuls have the same number of blocks. How many are in each handful now? How many blocks are left over? (1, 2 or 3 only. Why?)

Ask: If there are no blocks left over, what can you say?

The total number of blocks is divisible by 4

Ask: If there are blocks left over (1, 2 or 3), how many more blocks should you take from the bucket so that each handful will now have the same number with zero blocks left over. [Note: this is an introduction to the concept of mean.]

Name: _____

A.

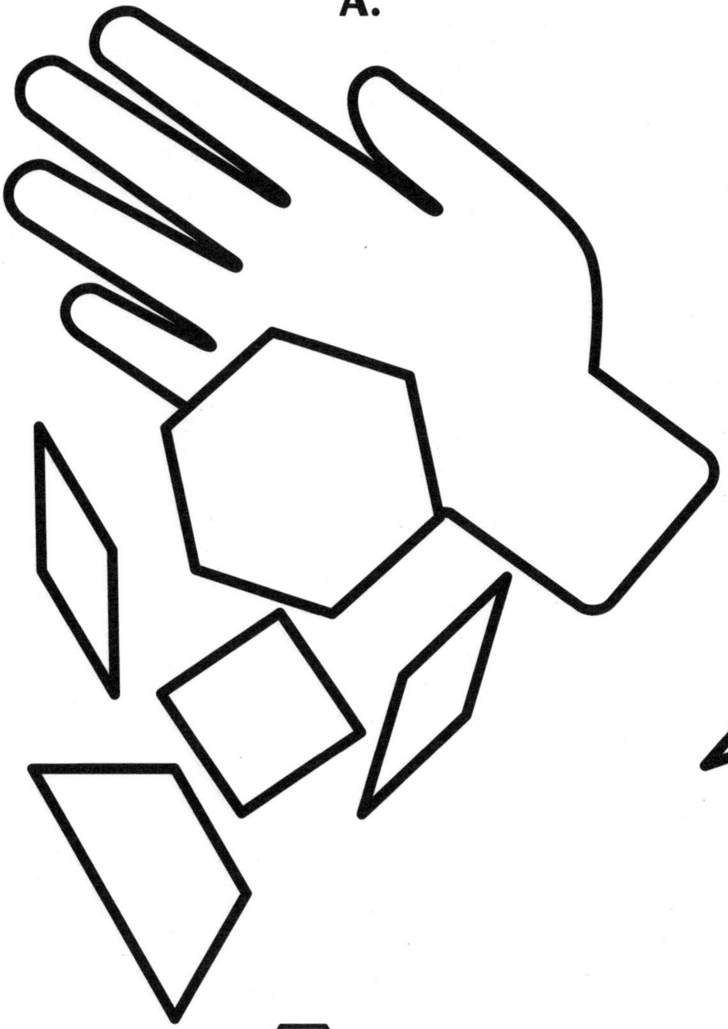

B.

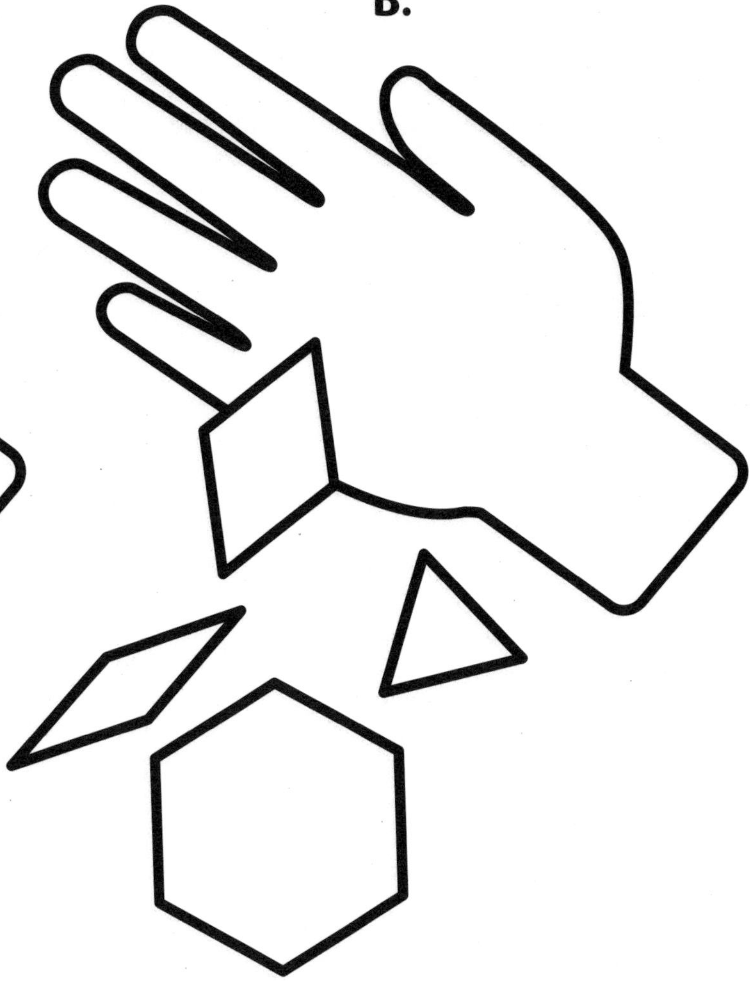

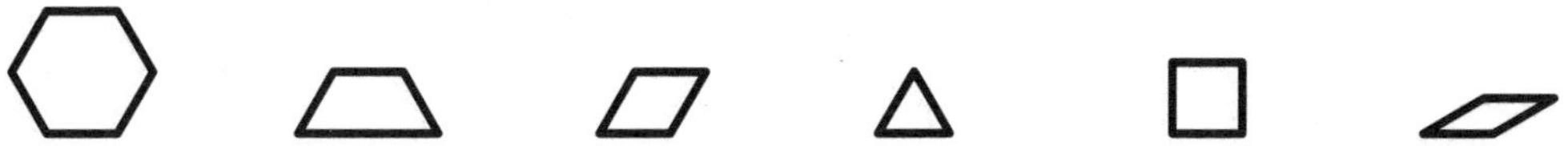

	⬡	⏢	▱	△	▢	▱	**Total**
Handful A							
Handful B							
Handful C							
Handful D							

Handful D estimate _ _ _ _ _ _

Focal Point

Probability – Describing parts of the data and the set of data as a whole to determine what the data shows.

Introduce the idea of likely outcomes.

Materials

- Four orange squares
- One blue rhombus
- A bag

Instructions/Guided Learning

This is an activity for a small group or the whole class to introduce probability.

Prepare a bag containing 5 pattern blocks (4 orange squares and one blue rhombus). Students do not know the exact contents. Shake the bag for the group.

1. There are only 5 blocks in total in the bag. There can only be blue rhombuses or orange squares. What could be in the bag?

   5 orange squares; 4 orange squares, 1 rhombus; 3 orange squares, 2 rhombuses

Ask the students to record their guesses on the line for My Prediction 1. Record all of the correct possibilities on the chalkboard and allow time for discussion.

Shake the bag and select one block and record it, making a tally, on the chalkboard next to a drawing of a square or rhombus. Return the block to the bag. Shake the bag and select another block. Perform this same action 5 times in all. After the first time, let a student shake the bag while you select the block (modeling for the class), recording each block on the chalkboard, and returning it to the bag. Ask the students to now make a prediction about the blocks on the line for My Prediction 2.

2. Did you change your prediction? Why?

You will now proceed with Experiment 1. Remove a block from the bag 10 times. The block must be returned to the bag after each trial. This time, let one student shake the bag and another student select a block (quickly, without feeling other blocks.) As you, the teacher, model the recording of the tally marks on the board, the students should make tally marks on their papers under Experiment 1. After doing this ask them to make another prediction (3).

3. Did you change your prediction? Why?

Experiment 2: the experiment continues as before for 10 more trials; students record tallies as before. They should write their final prediction on the line for My Prediction 4

4. Did you change your prediction this time? Why?

At the board, you should record the number of students choosing each of the 6 possibilities. After discussion, the secret of the bag is revealed.

Explore More with PB!

Ask: Was the orange square or the blue rhombus selected more often?

Ask: Why were we more likely to pick the orange square?

Ask: Did you make a better prediction after 5 trials or 25 trials? Why?

We need many trials to get a good estimate. Write in your math journal the "secret" and explain which block is more likely to be picked.

Secret Treasures

Name: _____

My Prediction 1 □ _____ ◇ _____

My Prediction 2 □ _____ ◇ _____

Experiment 1

_____
Tally

_____
Tally

My Prediction 3 □ _____ ◇ _____

Experiment 2

_____
Tally

_____
Tally

My Prediction 4 □ _____ ◇ _____

Focal Point

Probability – Describing parts of the data and the set of data as a whole to determine what the data shows.

Introduce the idea of likely outcomes.

Materials

- Orange squares
- Blue rhombuses
- Bags

Teacher places 5 blocks in a bag, chosen from only orange squares or blue rhombuses. Make up enough bags for every pair of students in the class. Students work in pairs.

Instructions/Guided Learning

Give one copy of the worksheet to each pair of students. Designate one student as student A and one as student B.

1. Orange squares and blue rhombuses were placed in the bags. Each bag has only 5 blocks. Guess how many of each kind of block is in your bag.

Tell students to make an initial prediction about what is in the bag and record it. Now they should do the experiments. For Experiment 1, there will be 10 trials. The students are to quickly remove only 1 block each time without feeling the other blocks. They will make a tally for each trial on the drawing of the correct block and return the block to the bag. When they have finished this, ask each of them to record a prediction based on the results on the line for My Prediction.

2. Did your estimate change? Why?

For Experiment 2, have the students do 20 trials. Once again, they should tally the results and make a final prediction. On line 4 tell them to write their estimate after discussing each student's predictions. Now they can take the blocks out of the bag and see if they were correct.

Explore More with PB!

Discuss how to make the contents of a bag so that the selection of an orange square would be certain; so that the selection of an orange square would be impossible; so that the selection of an orange square would be just as likely as the selection of a blue rhombus.

Name: _____

1. First Prediction   A ☐ _____   ◇ _____

B ☐ _____   ◇ _____

Experiment 1

 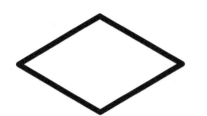

1. My Prediction   A ☐ _____   ◇ _____

B ☐ _____   ◇ _____

Experiment 2

 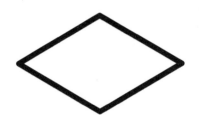

3. Final Prediction   A ☐ _____   ◇ _____

B ☐ _____   ◇ _____

4. We think our bag contains _____

5. We were correct!   or

We should have guessed   ☐ _____   ◇ _____

Focal Point

Statistics and Probability – Formulating conclusions and making predictions from experiments.

Materials

- Triangles
- Rhombuses
- A shoebox

Teacher places 7 blocks in a shoebox, choosing from only triangles and rhombuses.

Instructions/Guided Learning

From a bucket containing only triangles and rhombuses, place 7 blocks in a mystery shoebox.

1. Find what possible combinations of triangles and rhombuses there can be if you have exactly 7 blocks. One possible combination is 7 triangles and 0 rhombuses. Those numbers have been recorded on your worksheet.

2. List all possible combinations of triangles and rhombuses on your worksheet. Use your pattern blocks to help you find the combinations.

Review the fact that one rhombus is equivalent to 2 triangles.

3. If I replaced all the rhombuses with an equivalent number of triangles, the shoebox would contain 9 triangles. Which of the 8 possible combinations is the correct one?

2 rhombuses and 5 triangles

Explore More with PB!

In another shoebox of 7 total triangles and rhombuses, if the rhombuses were replaced with the equivalent number of triangles, the box would contain 13 triangles.

Ask: Which of the possible 8 combinations is the correct one?

6 rhombuses and 1 triangle

Name: _____

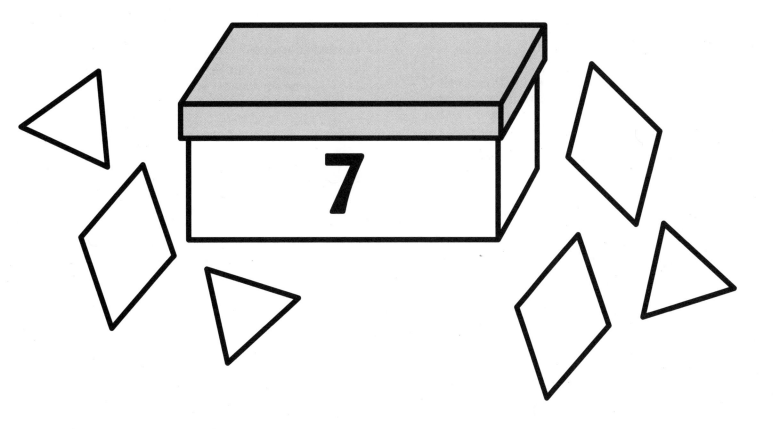

1. ___7___ △ and ___0___ ◇ were selected.
2. _____ △ and _____ ◇ were selected.
3. _____ △ and _____ ◇ were selected.
4. _____ △ and _____ ◇ were selected.
5. _____ △ and _____ ◇ were selected.
6. _____ △ and _____ ◇ were selected.
7. _____ △ and _____ ◇ were selected.
8. _____ △ and _____ ◇ were selected.

Focal Point

Statistics and Probability – Formulating conclusions and making predictions from experiments. Constructing and analyzing frequency tables, bar graphs, picture graphs and line plots, using them to solve problems.

Materials

- Triangles
- Trapezoids
- A shoebox

Teacher places 8 blocks in a shoebox, choosing from only triangles and trapezoids.

Instructions

Ask students to find what possible combinations there can be of triangles and trapezoids out of 8 blocks. One possible combination is 8 triangles and 0 trapezoids. Another combination is 1 triangle and 7 trapezoids. Those numbers have been recorded on the worksheet. Tell students to complete filling in the blanks, listing all 9 possible combinations.

When they are done with this, ask them to transfer the data into Table A as shown. When Table A is complete they will copy the first two columns from Table A to Table B. Then tell them to complete Table B showing the correct exchange of triangles for trapezoids (3 triangles for 1 trapezoid).

Guided Learning

1. How many possible combinations of blocks can be in the shoebox? Use your pattern blocks to help you find the combinations. The first two are done for you.

2. How many triangles are equivalent to one trapezoid?

   3 triangles

3. If I replaced all the trapezoids with the equivalent triangles, the box would contain 12 triangles. Which of the 8 possible combinations is the correct one?

   6 triangles and 2 trapezoids

Explore More with PB!

Have each student write his/her own mystery shoebox problem with the necessary clues, using only 6 blocks (triangles and trapezoids). Give the written solution.

Name: _____

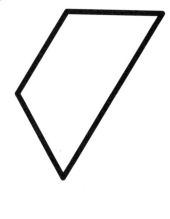

8 △ and

1. __0__ △ and __8__ ⬭

2. __1__ △ and __7__ ⬭

3. _____ △ and _____ ⬭

4. _____ △ and _____ ⬭

5. _____ △ and _____ ⬭

6. _____ △ and _____ ⬭

7. _____ △ and _____ ⬭

8. _____ △ and _____ ⬭

9. _____ △ and _____ ⬭

TABLE A

△	⬭	Total
0	8	8
1	7	8

TABLE B

△	⬭	⬭	Total △
0	8	24	24
1	7	21	22
2	6	18	
	5	15	18

Probability & Statistics: **All in the Family**

Materials

- Four squares
- One blue rhombus
- Three trapezoids
- Two hexagons

Instructions

Tell the students that for the first line, "hexagon," only 2 hexagons are in the group of pattern blocks. Therefore in the first column (BELONG), the Square, Rhombus and Trapezoid have been marked with an X and the Hexagon has a "2" in it. In the second column (DO NOT BELONG), the Hexagon has been eliminated and the number of Squares (4), Rhombuses (1) and Trapezoids (3) are indicated. The number of blocks that belong (in the family) total 2. The numeral 2 has been written in the "Total Belong" column. Tell the students that for each line they should separate the blocks into 2 groups, those that belong and those that do not belong. Each line poses a rule and the student should record their answers. Some of the subsets will be empty.

Note: In probability, "or" is inclusive, i.e., red blocks or blue blocks means you may count both red blocks AND blue blocks as a part of the subset.

Explore More with PB!

Review the numbers that belong and do not belong for each rule and note that the total is always 10 blocks.

Have students take any 12 pattern blocks, make two new rules and decide which blocks belong and which blocks do not belong. Remember the total (in the family) must be 12.

All in the Family

Name: _____

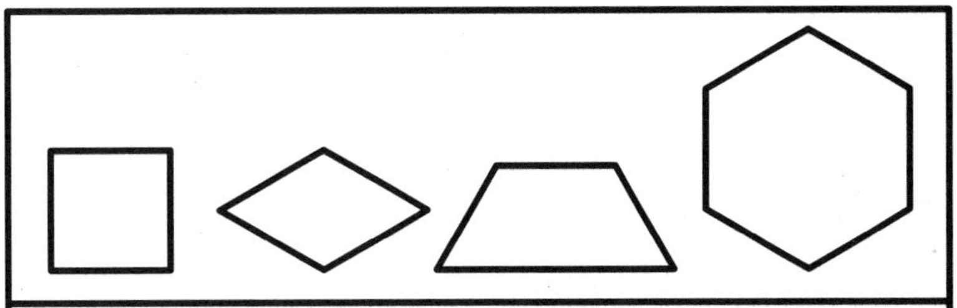

TAKE

| | 4 | 1 | 3 | 2 |

Rule	Belong	Do Not Belong	Total Belong
hexagon ⬡	⊠ ⊠ ⊠ ②	4 1 3 ⊠	2
red	▢ ◇ ⬠ ⬡	▢ ◇ ⬠ ⬡	
orange	▢ ◇ ⬠ ⬡	▢ ◇ ⬠ ⬡	
trapezoid ⬠	▢ ◇ ⬠ ⬡	▢ ◇ ⬠ ⬡	
blue	▢ ◇ ⬠ ⬡	▢ ◇ ⬠ ⬡	
red or blue	▢ ◇ ⬠ ⬡	▢ ◇ ⬠ ⬡	
quadrilaterals	▢ ◇ ⬠ ⬡	▢ ◇ ⬠ ⬡	
pattern blocks	▢ ◇ ⬠ ⬡	▢ ◇ ⬠ ⬡	
orange or green	▢ ◇ ⬠ ⬡	▢ ◇ ⬠ ⬡	
circle	▢ ◇ ⬠ ⬡	▢ ◇ ⬠ ⬡	

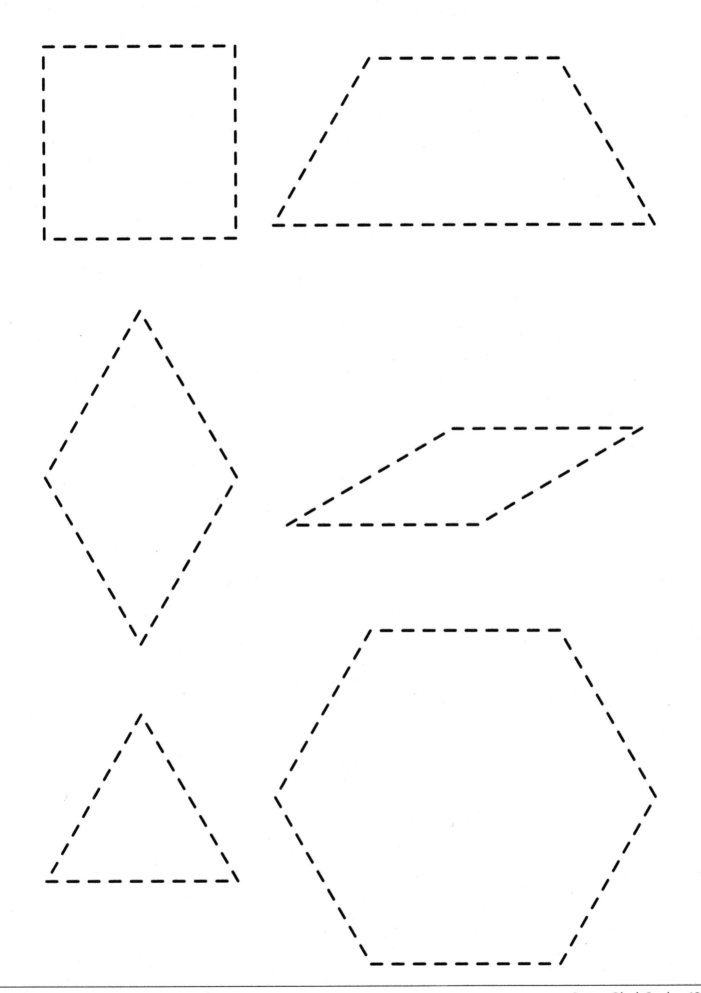